EDUCATION ka*

(Dream for Transforming Nations)

Dr. Chiranjib Kumar (PhD)
Professor – Author - Trainer

Dr. Opiew Cham (Ed.D)
Co-Author & Editor

*ka: (In ancient Egypt) supposed spiritual part of an individual human being or God, which survived (with the soul) after death and could reside in a statue of the person.

Copyright © Authors
All rights reserved. No part of this publication may be reproduced or transmitted, in any form or by any means, without permission. However data may be taken as reference for research work or teaching material (Lecture Notes) or training purpose with proper acknowledgement of authors/editors.

Disclaimer: The book is based on research work and views expressed in the articles/chapters are those of the authors and not necessarily of the publisher or Editor. References have been provided at the reference page.

First Printed: December' 2019
(Lulu Press, USA, www.lulu.com)

ISBN: 978-1-79478-303-4

DISCLAIMER

The views expressed in the book are those of the Authors only and not necessarily of the editors and publisher. The purpose of this book is not to hurt the sentiments, emotions and dignity of any person. Most of the *Illustrations* in the book have been kept as it is.

ACKNOWLEDGEMENT

We would like to thank all those people who have not only supported us but also given motivation to complete our book on time. We are deeply indebted to esteemed academics, authors, researchers and industry intellectuals for embarking with us on this book journey. Thank you for being our motivators and source of inspiration. Your contributions, comments and insights have been of great value to us. Thank to those entire respondent who have not only responded to our query and questionnaires on time but also assisted in data collection process in their own way.

This book would never been accomplished without cooperation from the industry and educationist therefore, we are grateful to all the professionals. A special thanks to Gambella University and MTC Global for providing us sufficient time, resources and ideas to fill the existed gap of information on dynamics of education through this book. This book would never been accomplished without cooperation from the publisher therefore, we are deeply indebted to our publisher for interest shown in publication.

Finally our greatest thank to parents and lovely family, you all are just wonderful and a source of continuous inspiration and motivation.

ABBREVIATIONS

AICTE: All India Council for Technical Education
AMA: American Marketing Association
CBSE: Central Board of Secondary Education
CGPA: Cumulative Grade Point Average
CMO: Chief Marketing Officer
ECTS: European Credit Transfer System
ISRO: Indian Space Research Organisation
MOOC: Massive Open Online Courses
MTC: Management Teachers Consortium
NAAC: National Assessment and Accreditation Council
NACE: National Accreditation Council for Education
NCERT: National Council of Educational Research and Training
NCTE: National Council for Teachers Education
NEET: National Eligibility and Entrance Test
NGO: Non-Governmental Organization
OBE: Outcome Based Education
UGC: University Grant Commission

PREFACE

Since a long time, education has been remained in focus area for the doctrine makers and preachers. Many times it posed many challenges and issues before reformers due to the varying geography and prevailing condition of region. Education is a driving force of world economy that could only help in sustainable development and conservation of scarce resource linked with environment. It has various forms and each form has its own significance and value in terms of human life and dynamic world. Education generates knowledge; thoughts; ideas; skills; kindness and humanity within human being that no one can steal until the possessor offer it to the seeker. It is like river that originates to serve the world. The book has tried to bring the dynamism in education by raising some serious issues and its solutions. Commodification and commercialization of education has posed education as luxury product in the world, which is beyond the capacity and reach of poor people. And rising inflation of daily use commodities has added a big barrier of getting it on time. Several questions have been raised while discussing the issues and challenges that need to be focused while reading the book. And if possible then must be solved immediately to avoid the long lasting negative impact of education.

Education should not be the reason of poverty in the world. And poverty should not be the reason of illiteracy in the world. The purpose of education must be oriented towards generating peace, prosperity, happiness, eligibility and employability with humanity.

It is well said, that if, you educate one man, you educate one man only but if, you educate one woman, you educate whole family.

Learning is Growth and Innovation is Process.

Author & Editor

Sl. NO.	CONTENTS	PAGE NO.
	Acknowledgement	*4*
	Abbreviations	*5*
	Preface	*6-7*
	Content	*8-9*

1. EDUCATION IN GLOBAL SCENARIO (11-18)

2. CONCEPT OF EDUCATION (20-37)

- Nature of education is divine
- Concept of learning
- Literacy strategies
- Views and opinion of teachers, authors and researchers

3. DIMENSIONS OF EDUCATION (39-47)

- seven dimensions

4. MORAL EDUCATION (49-68)

5. VALUE BASED EDUCATION (70-86)

- Components of Value Based Education
- Education and Training In Non-Violence should be Part of the Curriculum
- Belief in Legacy

6. HOLISTIC EDUCATION (88-99)

- Does education fills or kills?

- Prayer : Perspective Of Education

7. EDUCATION SYSTEM IN THE WORLD

- Teacher is not the sage on the stage
- Library **(88 – 99)**
- Increased monitoring
- Cellphones Get A Ringing Endorsement In Classrooms

8. SUSTAINABLE EDUCATION (101-135)

9. EDUCATION MODELS (150-156)

10. FRAMEWORK TO IMPLEMENT (158-174)

11. HI-TECH EDUCATION AND SMART EDUCATION (176- 186)

- Applications of Technology in Education
- Technology Disadvantages
- EDUTECH: The Future of India Education

12. EDUCATION TOURISM (188 -189)

13. CONCLUSION AND ROAD MAP (191-197)

ANNEXURE- I Cell Phone Etiquette **199**

REFERENCES 202 -204

(page purposely kept blank)

Chapter

1. EDUCATION IN GLOBAL SCENARIO

Education has become costly affairs instead of awakening affairs in this fast moving globalised world. The concept of education has been changing drastically from "Dark to Light" to" Dare to Dream" since for the past three decades. Time is not too far when the main objective of education would become "Objective" rather than "Subjective and Holistic". Fast globalised world has dug big cannon for the immersion of glory and antiquity of education due to which only ambiguity would be left in education to offer. Political infiltration and interference has already spoiled the recipe of dynamic education with no space for dynamism. Modern philosophies have almost killed the power of "Learning" and now factor *"L"(Listening)* is missing from education. Only "Earning" left with. One should never forget that, if we focus on "earning" then it will bring wealth with *Clashes, Conflicts (2C) and Insecurity (1I)*. Learning is most important factor in education. It means factor "L", that can be added only through the real environment, realistic teachers, institutions, schools, colleges and universities or participating in conclave, conference, webinar, , video conference, seminar and holistic lecture sessions where teachers (preachers or counselors) offer it.

Freedom of education and its flow should not be stopped at one enclosed premise, rather than it should scattered beyond the boundaries of *Inequality, Inseperability, Inadequacy, Infirmity and Insecurity (5 Is)* leading to *Integrity and Interdependency (2 Is)*.

Transformation, Transfusion, Transmission and Transcending (4T) are the important characteristics of education system. These four pillars are the foundation and fundamentals of education system, avoiding it may result as serious consequences that would further led atmosphere of anonymity. The goal of education need not to be restricted upto *"Learning" or adding "L"* to *"earning"* only. Instead it should be beyond the limit of limitations and demarcation. Creating models; embarking improvement; measuring performance; smart class rooms ; hi-tech infrastructures; dynamic research; multifaceted development ; and other variables in education would be of no use if, "holistic" approach of education is missing from everywhere.

The key questions in present scenarios are,

Q. Do we really think about education and educating people or it just a rumour for gaining short term respect and long term business?

Q. Do we really focus on value based education or is it simply a myth to fool the world?

Q. Do we have a proper definition of value based holistic education?

Q. How do we know the overall scenario of education?

Q. How to regain and retain the lost glory and antiquity of education?

Q. What kind of framework would be helpful in getting objective to be fulfilled?

Q. How to design, develop and implement it?

Thousands of such type of questions knocked our doors every time whenever we think about education in its prevailed conditions.

Diversification and diversities are good in education as it brings innovations but not by killing its value.

It's not too late to start thinking about the magnitude of education in transforming nations in sustainable ways. Education should not be the reasons of mass destructions and demolition. It can't be used as a weapon of sanity. It has lost its path that need to be redirected. Teacher and student relationship must be in line with value (morale), knowledge, learning, sharing and caring (differentiating between good and bad things). Providing education in natural surrounding and settings perhaps the best way through which the dream of sustainable education can be achieved. Education must include the constituents of environmental sustainability that are Reduce, Reuse and Recycle.

There are some mindboggling questions that must be considered while designing and delivering the sustainable education.

Q. How to overcome with the hypothesis of good education and bad education?

Q. What is sustainable education?

Q. Is sustainable education is synonyms of holistic education?

According to G Madhavan Nair(Former chairman of ISRO,India), Education in world has become a commercial commodity. The tendency of political parties to make college campuses a training ground for budding politicians. No real education was happening at the campuses and students were being assessed on their ability to memorize topics rather than on their ability to understand concepts of a subject.

Q. Why the education system has deteriorated considerably?

Result is that the people who come out even after graduation or engineering, they are not employable. They don't have the basic understanding of the subject; don't have the skills for applying knowledge for practical applications and this is resulting in a pathetic situation."

Quality of education has become the first casualty at many private institutions whose prime aim seems to be to increase student intake and make money. Basically education has become a commercial commodity these days rather than acquiring excellence in knowledge and value."

Some institutes and universities in the world have been maintaining its rank and reputation till now, but mostly because these institutes grab the best of talent. However, even these institutes needed to improve the quality of education to make an impactful mark from the global perspective through maintaining sustainable development and holistic approach.

Politics and education should not be mixed with each other. There are many political parties who want to use educational institutions for building up their cadres rather than ideal citizen with value based education, and that should be stopped. Instead of influencing students on campus, political parties should start a separate institute for training politicians.

The focal point of education should be improvement of observation, analytical, and communication skills of students, with a leaning toward cultivating moral values.

These should form the basis of primary education. Once the foundation is strong and shows them the way how to acquire knowledge, which is sufficient. There is no point in just doing 10,000 answers by-heart that will not take you anywhere. Education system should be an enabler, that kind of change is required.

The lack of talented people in the teaching profession and added that those who were in the profession are not being given proper and professional training.

Quality must have in the teaching profession and every teacher also needed to be evaluated periodically. Adopting basic lessons from 'Gurukul system' particularly a strong personal relation between the teacher-student and the parent kind of ambience need to be created. Evaluations should not be based on annual exam. It should be constant evaluation where the parent also participates in a very scientific manner. Moral studies have to be given strong base in early part of education.

The three language (National Language, International Language (English), and local language) policy and said that it should be adopted in all the states.

National language is a link language, English has become mandatory for our system, and basic education can be imparted in a much more efficient manner in local language.

Emphasizing on the scientific nature of language, students must be given an option to study in respective language.

Education must have power to breed *Love, Affinity and Humanity (LAH)* among people including of knowledge and skills. Simply providing education would be of no value if aforesaid components are missing from the beginning of imparting education. Education must try to differentiate in between inhuman and human. Generating awareness about the presence of "cerebrum" in human body and its superb power of imagination perhaps could be the best ideal way to take education further in sustainable direction.

The real craftsmanship in education would be to eradicate the shaft of fear through shaft of inspiration, like a shaft of moonlight fell on the lake.

(page purposely kept blank)

Chapter

2. CONCEPT OF EDUCATION

The concept of education is basically based on the theory of learning or preaching where educators, preachers or mentors(teachers) makes sure that students, disciple or devotee are devoted to listen or grasped the master or followed the mentor. Deaf, dumb and blind anyone can learn, provided this teacher (mentor) and learner must have interest and commitment to be educated (trained) and learned respectively. Education doesn't require classroom, institutions and universities, only teacher is sufficient with interest in learner to intake manifold tasks. Education has paved its own way to reach to the ultimate seeker.

Nature of education is divine. It means no space and scope for bad elements or evil. Hence those involved in preaching or teaching unruly, inhuman, unjustified, ill manners, insane and vulnerable things cannot claim it as education because by nature education is divine only.

There could be only one aspect of education, "showing the truth" that is correct path of living in sustainable way. Education appeals for liability and credibility in co-relation with sustainability of environment where it persists. Even *one drop of education can bring the shaft of light in darkness of dormant mind to awake the soul.*

The function of education is like lightning a lamp.

A good researcher has the potential to be a good teacher. Now it depends upon the researcher what attracts him more - research or teaching. But when teaching is supported with research, the taught is mesmerised by whatever is taught by the teacher. It is called soul to soul teaching. Vomiting information many times does not work on the taught.

Dr. S. Radhakrishnan (former president of India) is considered among the best teacher in India. Naturally, he might have been a good researcher coupled with good observer. These two traits - research and testing what is researched in real life that is observing and applying those researches makes a person good teachers.

The link will continue to exist so long as faculty doing research also show earnestness in classrooms; if research is esoteric then it will lose relevance; somehow there is a feeling that those who are excessively inclined to do research seldom do justice in classrooms; research must be a tool to improve pedagogy and teaching methods; today"s students are intelligent and they can easily discern between a sincere effort and a not so sincere effort.

We assume whatever is of foreign is gold, ours is scrap. The mind formed on a foreign land with foreign education can hardly allow a person to think out of box, mainly in the context of native country's soil/real needs.

Many leaders speak in terms of local conditions, but when it comes for implementation they brought foreign concepts like semester, CGPA, ECTS, Choice Based Credit System (CBCS), OBE, without judging their utility to the native soil. Unless we do not throw away this yoke on our neck, I fear, nothing wishful would happen in any country. One has to peep deep into the history and present scenario.

Educators at all levels need to ask,

Q. Are we and our systems really learning oriented or teaching oriented?

Q. Are we student friendly?

Q. Do we support student welfare?

It will be an uphill task to grapple with these issues, but it is worth putting the efforts rather than producing substandard professionally qualified persons. We have to agree that there is *"No gain without Pain"*.

According to Sadhuguru (2017), today, the world is no longer about people; it is about the economic engine we have built. It has become bigger than us and we are afraid to stop it even for a moment, so we have to keep the engine going all the time. Unfortunately, education has mostly become about manufacturing cogs for this machine. We can't let the machine fail, so our children have become the spare parts and fuel needed to keep it running.

There are studies which say that if a child goes through twenty years of formal education and comes out with a Ph.D, seventy percent of his intelligence is irrevocably destroyed. Essentially, we have mistaken information for education. If you deaden the brain with too much information, the possibility of intelligence is definitely lost. What we accumulate and who we are should remain separate. Who I am should not be influenced by what I have accumulated – whether it is material objects, information or impressions.

Don't Mistake Intellect for Intelligence

The purpose of education is to expand the horizons of individual human beings. But that is definitely not happening in most places right now. As people get educated, they really can't get along with anyone! Those who are not so educated can live together. But once you become educated, you become isolated because that is the nature of the intellect. And education today is entirely intellect-based. There is no other dimension of intelligence in it. Mistaking intellect for intelligence is a serious error. *It is like trying to drive your car on a single wheel instead of all four.*

Intellect can function only with the backing of your memory. Or in other words, your intellect functions with accumulated information. If your memory is removed, your intellect is quite useless by itself. But there are other dimensions of intelligence within you that do not need the support of memory. If education systems do not focus on activating these dimensions of intelligence, you will create a workforce but no geniuses.

The Best People Should Go Into Teaching

But more than the systems themselves, we have to upgrade those who deliver the system. If we do this, every system will work well. If we are interested in the future generations, the best people in the world must go into teaching. What a child needs is inspiration, not just information. We need to completely take away the idea of instruction from the teaching process.

You think you need to instruct someone only if you have assumed they are of a lower intelligence than yourself, which is a serious mistake. There is sufficient scientific data to show that a thirty-year-old is not as intelligent as a child before he even enters school. The only reason we look smart is because we have more information than the child, which we try to show off through instruction. Instead of instruction, we need to empower teachers to inspire and transmit what really matters to them. Then, a child would surely sit up and listen, and every school system could become a fruitful process.

Intelligence need not be influenced, it needs to be inflamed. The purpose of education is to decondition intelligence, so that it becomes active, adapting to situations and doing what is appropriate. That is the essence of intelligence. But today, education systems are trying to condition the intelligence one way or the other. If human intelligence applies itself, every little thing will explode into a new cosmos by itself. This is what a human being is here for – to enhance life in a way that no other creature can. But right now, the only thing that is important is what serves our economic engine. What will earn you more money has become the fundamental question. If we do not remove this from our education system, there will only be a manufacturing unit, not education.

Education is not a production line. It is an organic happening. You cannot create an education system independent of the society in which we exist.

Q. Are we as a society willing to cultivate an eco-system suitable for a child to grow up in the best possible way?

This is a question all of us should ask ourselves.

Q. Are we going to do what we like to do, or are we going to be conscious of how every action of ours will impact future generations?

It is very important that we look at this because educating a child is not just a teacher's, parent's or school's business – it is the responsibility of the entire society.

Concept Of Learning

Learning Concept (Prof. Bholanath Dutta, President, MTC Global)

1. Self-directed learning

2. Learning through play

3. Scenario-based learning

4. Game-based learning

5. Project-based learning

6. Peer-to-Peer instruction

7. School-to-school instruction (using Skype in the classroom, for example)

8. Learning through projects

9. Problem-based learning

10. Challenge-based learning

11. Inquiry-based learning

12. Mobile learning

13. Gamified learning (gamification)

14. Cross-curricular projects

15. Reciprocal Teaching

16. "Flipped-class" learning

17. Face-to-Face Driver blended learning

18. Rotation blended learning

19. Flex Blended Learning

20. "Online Lab" blended learning

21. Sync Teaching

23. HyFlex Learning

24. Self-guided MOOC

25. Traditional MOOC

26. Competency-Based Learning

27. Question-based learning

Literacy Strategies

28. Write-Around

29. Four Corners

30. Accountable Talk

31. RAFT Assignments

32. Fishbowl

33. Debate

34. Gallery Walk

35. Text Reduction

36. Concentric Circles

37. Traditional Concept-Mapping (teacher-given strategy–"fishbone" cause-effect analysis, for example)

38. Didactic, Personalized Concept Mapping (student designed and personalized for their knowledge-level and thinking patterns)

39. Mock Trial

40. Non-academic video + "academic" questioning

41. Paideia Seminar

42. Symposium

43. Socratic Seminar

44. QFT Strategy

45. Concept Attainment

46. Directed Reading Thinking Activity

47. Paragraph Shrinking

48. FRAME Routine

49. Jigsaw Strategy

50. Content-Based Team-Building Activities

Views And Opinion Of Teachers, Authors And Researchers-

1) Knowledge and experience are also cumulative. Education is one of the important vehicles for learning. In the end, life is about learning more about us, our strengths and weaknesses. The ultimate goal of education: Liberalization, Salvation, realization, Nirvan, Mukti, Enlightenment, the Day of Judgment, Wisdom, etc. Stamping it just Spirituality and forget all about it is not expected.

As time passes, we start filtering out the non-essential from the essential. Some call this as an experience; others call it wisdom or enlightenment (Nagi K, MTC Global).

2) All our problems tend to gather under two questions about knowledge: Having the ability and desire to know, how and what should we learn? And, having learned, how and for what should we use what we know?"--*Wendell Berry, America's greatest living writer.*

3) Man is made up of three things: Body, mind and soul (spirit). In Vedanta we come across four terms:

- Manas: Sensory, processing mind.
- Chitta: Storage of impressions.
- Buddhi: Knows, decides, judges, and discriminates.
- Ahankara: "I-maker", egoity.

Learning is a process that goes within the mind, grasping, understanding, consolidation, etc., may be considered either the components of learning or synonymous with learning. Learning is a natural/divine gift given to either animate or inanimate things (for survival) the Nature has created. Springs, hysteresis loop of elastic material or permanent deformation in a plastic state, etc. are found in nature. Present learning machines is a part of that, man-made. In fact, habit is formed as a result of re-practicing the same thing many times and it becomes the very nature of our body material! Learning cannot be trust but it happens knowingly or unknowingly. In both the cases soul is the driving force that propels mind and mind in turn propels the body. Thus, the chemistry of learning is somewhat so to say a mysterious thing! Training and education, the external agencies, man-made, are hopefully expected to promote learning. The faster one learns better. Of course the speed of learning is a function of age, diet, culture, etc. In fact, save man no other living creature is after external means like education and training (*Waghodekar,P' 2018*).

4) One more term: Grasping or Quick Grasping is equally important in the Learning Process. And the grasping is quicker when the mind is blooming - a younger age. You will find that youngsters (even 5th & 6th Graders) through experiments are

able to know many functions and features of Mobile Phones, Laptops & I-pads. Also a person who takes Learning Classes for Driving a four Wheeler would have slower reflexes compared to youngsters. I myself started learning to Drive a 4 Wheeler when I received my Tata Nano. I got the delivery of the first Lot in 2009 and had to urgently enroll to learn driving. At the same time my elder son who was in Xth standard - he took driving lessons within our campus from government vehicle drivers whereas I was having a 45 minutes lesson in a Private Driving School. My son had to wait for 4 years to get his very own License but he was already a better driver than me and my navigator prompting me when we were on road.

So it is true that to grasp and learn quickly you need quick mind reflexes. Wisdom will come at a later stage which will help in drafting the Will. There is also a very old adage: "JACK of All Arts, Master of None". No doubt in Modern competitive world, one needs to be ahead of others in the rat race and should have the ability to grasp opportunities coming your way. Education is a set curriculum taking you and putting you through paces in a subject or field voluntarily chosen to be pursued. Whereas Learning is a broad term where if you have an inclination and interest in a wide field of activities, you can continue to add to your knowledge of that field through theory and practice. Most Management Schools for that reason incorporate 'Summer Internship' (minimum 8 weeks) to enable the students to translate their theories into practical applications which is a process of Educational Learning. With more vistas and avenues of Learning opening up through World Wide Web, education is now becoming Commercial but at the same time it offers people with interest the choice of pursuing their area of interest even from the comfort of their homes (*Stephen N.' 2018, MTC Global*).

5) "Learning is like tasting samples of all sweet meats in a shop. I then decide what I like and what not."

Frankly I would love to get lost in a sweet meat shop at weekend so that I can sample through all the wares before coming to a confusion of which sweet was the best...maybe a couple of more rounds. How melancholic-yet true!(*Reddy,S'2018 MTC Global*).

6) As age and experience grows, we learn to leave the non-essential and focus our mental and motor energy on the essential. To me learning is like tasting samples of all sweet meats in a shop. I then decide what I like and what not. The open mindedness, risk taking and curiosity is learning. Years ago a rolling stone gathered no moss- today we need moss of multi hues and shapes to succeed. This constant ability to adjust the gear is learning. We need to learn everything-bit coins, cloud computing to politics. And then the mind knows what it wants-the insatiable need to know will direct what I learn, if I can learn without

trying to get a monetary benefit out of it. So learning is of two kinds-in depth knowledge of one topic or the knowledge of much and in depth of some. The choice is ours. I did Entrepreneurship for a lark twenty years ago. No use till in 2016 I used it to teach rural women entrepreneurship. When and how we use -and for what -we will never know. But I think beyond all these questions and concerns is one predominant factor: does it give you enormous joy doing the learning? If it does well there's a reason that is coming down your path and you wait for it. My love for temples, for understanding the soul's journey led me to learn about them in great depth. I do it for my soul.

Age I think has nothing to do with it. I remember my octo and nano parents as avid readers-the need to know and comprehend kept their minds razor sharp. And the ability to learn and the love of learning is a gift from heaven (S*ankar, Usha, MTC Global)*.

But the most important out of all the above points regarding learning is adding of factor "L" (Listening) to "Earn"(knowledge/skill/values) than only it would become "Learning". People in these days mostly focus on "earn" (money) rather than learn. The difference between Learn and Earn is only the letter "L" which makes a great sense.

(Page purposely kept blank)

Chapter 3. DIMENSIONS OF EDUCATION

Education has varying dimensions and each dimension has its own effect and impact on learning environment. These dimensions further depend on situations, scenario and socio-economic conditions of people, place and political system of area. The dimensions of education can be categorized broadly into seven categories.

I. Holistic Dimensions- *focused on integrating man and nature.*
II. Sustainable Dimensions – *focused on Preservation & Conservation.*
III. Experiential Dimensions- *focused on Research & Development.*
IV. Exponential Dimensions – *focused on Speed, Acceleration and Growth.*
V. Ethical Dimensions- *focused on code of ethics/guiding principles.*
VI. Value & Moral Dimensions- *focused on honour and respect, compassion*

VII. Learning Dimension- *the last but not least, focused on earning all the above dimensions through learning.*

All the above dimensions are interrelated and vital for the overall growth and development of education in the world. The learning atmosphere must consist of all the important dimensions to reach at the ultimate level of satisfaction that is production of mentor rather than a simple graduate, researcher, scientist, teacher, engineer, doctor or just any professional.

The main objective of any education should be to produce "a farmer" rather than "consumer" only.

Any education system must operate under the guidance of aforesaid framework and each of the above dimensions must be measured as per their set parameters and specified objectives. Learners and teachers must be evaluated as per the set dimensions and its effect and impact on education seekers and his friends.

A teacher must evaluate himself/herself whether he fits into "mentor" or just teacher only.

Illustration - 3.1

Why Higher Education Institutions Need CMOs

(Source: Forbes, Author, Kimberly A Whitler)

It's arguable that there is no industry where the marketing function is in a greater state of flux than higher education. Elizabeth Scarborough, CEO and Partner of SimpsonScarborough, a leading research, strategy, and creative services firm used by academic institutions across the U.S., indicates: "Less than two decades ago, marketing within higher education was a service function rather than a strategic function that drives admissions, recruitment, and fundraising. Few institutions had marketers and those that did rarely leveraged the expertise of marketers to help recruit better quality faculty and staff, admit higher quality students, or increase fundraising."

However, this is changing fast. I recently spoke at the AMA's CMO-only event where the rise of the CMO in higher education was chronicled. There is good news and bad news. In an analysis from the CMO Impact Study that compared higher ed

CMOs to their non-higher ed counterparts, turnover in the CMO position is much lower (and stability is much higher) in higher education institutions (see below). However, on the flip side, a challenge that CMOs in higher education have to manage is the lack of "customer centricity" within their organizations. In a question regarding the degree to which their organization is "driven by customer needs," the average CMO in higher education gave a rating of 3.53 versus 4.54 for CMOs in non-higher education organizations (higher rating is better). Although the sample size was small, it provides some directional insight into the benefits (stability) and challenges (lack of customer orientation) that higher education CMOs face.

Below, I share some insight from the AMA conference regarding why higher education institutions need cabinet-level marketers today and what this means for the future of the CMO role in higher education. For insight as to how this impact today's higher education CMO, I turned to three experts: Julie Daum, Executive Director, Communication and Marketing, University of Virginia Darden School of Business; Shari Gibbons, CMO at Woodbury University; and Teri Lucie Thompson, SVP for University Relations and CMO at University of Arizona. .

Q: Why is Marketing important in higher education institutions today?

Woodbury suggests: "The world is changing more rapidly than most colleges or universities can adapt to and yet, the competition for prospective students is getting fierce. The standard recruiting play-book no longer works and institutions will need to use marketing to clearly articulate their unique value proposition and tell their brand story. Hopefully that story is authentic and speaks to the competitive white space in the marketplace. Selling an undifferentiated product in this environment will get you nowhere."

Daum elaborates on the shift: "The internet and digital and social media have changed the way people discover and select educational programs. As marketers in higher education, we need to meet today's savvy students where they are and demonstrate to them the value that our institution brings. An education is a substantial investment, and we must earn their attention and interest. Institutions that embrace technology, leverage insights from marketing and data analysis, and develop a nimble and customer-focused marketing culture will be better equipped to attract great people to their schools and build lifelong connections to them."

Q: How will the CMO role change in the future?

Thompson indicates that right now, there are multiple tests happening around the country with the results yet to be determined. If marketers excel and make a difference, there should continue to be a steep increase in the number and importance of CMOs. If marketers brought in from outside of academia do not add value, then there will be a shift in hiring that reflects that learning. At present, CMOs can shape the role; key advantages seasoned CMOs bring to higher education include a brand management orientation, a data-driven decision-making and resource allocation orientation, and a focus on marketing as a strategic activity.

Q: How will the changing landscape of higher education impact the CMO?

Thompson indicates that there is a belief among some that the number of higher education institutions in the U.S. will have to dramatically decrease because of: 1) funding issues, 2) more competitive global marketplace for students (Asian countries are investing heavily in higher education), and 3) innovation in lower cost, alternative methods of acquiring an education (e.g., online, MOOCS, etc.) which may incent students to opt out of traditional education. In aggregate, these changes will increase the degree of competition, making the need for marketing excellence even more salient.

There is also another factor that can influence the hiring / status of marketing within higher education – the individuals hired to be President of the University and/or Deans of Business Schools. Historically, Presidents and Deans have risen through the faculty ranks. However, there is an emerging trend to hire presidents and especially business school Deans from outside of academia. In "The American President Study," by the American Council on Education (2012), Bryan Cook notes, "The share of [university] presidents whose immediate prior position was outside higher education has increased since 2006 from 13 percent to 20 percent." Consider Mitch

Daniels, the prior President of North American Operations for Eli Lilly and Governor of Indiana hired to be the President of Purdue University. Or Janet Napolitano who transitioned from Governor of Arizona to Director of Homeland Security to President of the University of California system. Kerry Murphy Healey, once Lieutenant Governor of Massachusetts now serves as President of Babson.

And there are even more examples of Deans having come from outside of academia: Suffolk University's William O'Neill (from Ford and Polaroid), Wake Forest University's Steve Reinemund (prior CEO and Chairman of PepsiCo), Chapman University's Reginald Gilyard (prior Managing Director of BCG consulting group), and the newly appointed Dean for the University of Virginia's Darden School of Business (Scott C. Beardsley from McKinsey & Co.). When Universities hire presidents and deans from industries that have seen the benefit of more sophisticated marketing, there is a greater likelihood that they may embrace the CMO role – particularly the skills that CMOs can offer higher education.

Only time will tell what the future holds for higher education CMOs. For right now, it is the wild west of CMO opportunities, a place where strong leaders with an ability to navigate bureaucracy can chart a new course and make a real difference.

(page purposely kept blank)

Chapter

4. MORAL EDUCATION

Moral education is the back bone of any education system that believes in raising morale (eternal peace) of learners. It must be the important goal of any education institution or practitioners to develop the good character within education seeker (learner). The old moral stories can be the best ways to enhance the character of learners. Even old scriptures and epics could play an important role in developing morale among learners. The major questions are,

Q. What is moral education?

Q. Does it have power to boost the morale of learners?

Illustration -4.1

Washington Post: Are teachers professional?

It seems like a simple question with an obvious answer, but for years teachers have been treated by policymakers as anything but professionals. Their judgments about how to educate and evaluate children are not taken into account, and they are evaluated by measures that statisticians say aren't valid assessment tools (such as when teachers are evaluated by the standardized test scores of students they don't have and subjects they don't teach). Teaching is often deemed "a calling," which is a way of saying that teachers are born and that teaching doesn't really require rigorous training beyond knowing the subject being taught.

Teaching is an occupation with a purpose of life.

A career in teaching starts as a bread and butter but as one grows it must end as a mission.

It is beyond the scope of words like professional or any other.

Occupation: A person's usual or principal work or business especially as a means of earning living, a vocation or calling.

Professional: One who follows an occupation as a means of livelihood or for gain.

Missionary: A person strongly in favor of a program, a set of principles, etc., who attempts to persuade or converts others.

Teaching, that persuades or converts others, falls in the category of missionary work. Hence, teaching could be termed as an occupation with a life mission. There is no denying of the fact that to become successful in any occupation, perfection, efficiency self-transformation is a must. Mission calls for sacrifice and/or self-less service; and it is not for only earning one's living or for gain.

Illustration -4.2 Review of Case Study

(Source: Professor John Hattie, Director, Melbourne Educational Research Institute, The University of Melbourne)

Professor Hattie's work is internationally acclaimed. His influential 2008 book Visible Learning: A synthesis of over 800 Meta-Analyses Relating to Achievement is believed to be the world's largest evidence-based study into the factors which improve student learning. Involving more than 80 million students from around the world and bringing together 50,000 smaller studies, the study found positive teacher-student interaction is the most important factor in effective teaching.

Myth: Teaching at private schools is better than teaching at public schools

Reality: Professor Hattie says research suggests this is not true. When it comes down to the quality of teachers, it's very, very hard to find evidence that there is any major difference between public and private schools in terms of the growth, the value that teachers add. In fact it's almost a myth to believe they're that different. You get some of the best teachers in Australia in some of our poorest school areas. What really matters is good leadership within a school, and how teachers are selected and developed, no matter whether it is private or government.

Myth: How much you spend on your child's education equates to how well they will do at school

Reality: Evidence shows that it is the quality of teaching that matters most. Professor Hattie says parents can choose schools, and choose to pay private school fees, but they can't choose their child's teachers. There is no linear relationship between what you might spend on a child and the education outcome for the child.

Myth: Homework is a necessary evil

Reality: Meta-analysis has shown that the amount of homework a student does in primary school has no effect on student achievement or progress. The research is not saying that there should be no homework, but if schools are going to set homework (which many parents expect) then the focus should be on the type of homework given. Homework does have more effect on results for secondary school children, but generally students are given way too much. A short time spent practising what was taught that day can have the same effect as one or two hours of study. Professor Hattie says what happens in the classroom is what matters most. Five to 10 minutes practising what was taught at school that day has the same effect as one to two hours studying something different. The worst thing you can do with homework is give young kids projects to do.

Myth: Reducing class size leads to better outcomes for students

Reality: Reducing class size can enhance student achievement but generally the effect is only marginal. What really matters is that the teacher is effective and having an impact, no matter what size the class is. Professor Hattie says the preoccupation with class size is an enigma; what's really important is that the teacher learns to be an expert in their own class, no matter what size it is.

Myth: We should be happy if our children are 'doing their best'

Reality: Not so. Professor Hattie says telling a student to 'do your best' is the worst thing a teacher or parent can do. Some of the most effective learning happens when teachers ask students what they predict their results will be before a test. Upon establishing a student's expectations of their own abilities, a successful teacher will challenge them by saying they can do better. What a student achieved yesterday should never be okay tomorrow.

Myth: Teachers should be experts on their subject and do most of the talking in class

Reality: Most teachers talk between 80 and 90% of the time during a lesson. The research has shown that students are more engaged and learn more when teachers talk around 50% of the time, or even less. Evidence shows that children can learn very effectively from their peers; when another student explains concepts to them. The best teachers encourage their students to be active and engaged in the classroom, exploring ideas, and not just passively listening.

Myth: Wearing a school uniform has a positive impact on students' results

Reality: Research has found wearing a uniform has no impact at all on educational outcomes. Professor Hattie says conversations about school uniforms are distracting; it doesn't matter if uniform is compulsory or not as it makes no difference whatsoever to student achievement. A school should decide whether they want to enforce a uniform or not but waste no further time debating it.

Myth: Academic achievement of secondary school students is better at single sex schools

Reality: Professor Hattie says research has found that co-educational school students perform the same as single sex schools

Myth: Extra-curricular activities distract and diminish school performance

Reality: Professor Hattie says extra-curricular activities are actually powerful in terms of helping children learn. The best predictor of health, wealth and happiness in adult life is not academic achievement at school but the number of years schooled; extra-curricular activities can be a fun and inviting way to get children to enjoy school and want to spend more time there learning.

Myth: TV has a negative effect on a child's learning progress

Reality: Not directly. Professor Hattie says the problem with a child watching too much television is that it stops them from spending that time learning in more productive ways, such as by reading or developing their communication and relationship skills.

Myth: A child's birth date can have a negative impact on learning

Reality: Professor Hattie has found that the date which a child's birthday falls in the school year has an effect on their progress initially, as there is a big difference in the ability of a child who is 5 years 1 month and one who is 5 years 11 months. However, no difference is found after two to three years of schooling. What has a more dramatic effect on a child's academic achievements is whether a child makes a friend in their first month at school.

Myth: Children Learn Best When They Discover Things On Their Own

Reality: The idea that children learn best when they discover things on their own is well entrenched in the minds of many educators – but it is a myth. Professor Hattie says this theory is not based on evidence. Research shows that when teachers actively teach kids, they have more than three times more effect on students' results than when simply facilitating learning. While we want our students to become free-thinking, independent citizens leaving them to learn independently is not the way to do this.

Myth: Children Learn More When They Have Control Over Their Learning

Reality: This is another popular theory that has no grounding in evidence. It's called student-centred learning and Professor Hattie says it has been blindly accepted by many educators as a good idea. Rather than having the teacher decide what students will learn, advocates of student-centred learning believe that you need to be guided by students' interests. The idea is that giving students choices about what they learn helps them to learn more effectively. It doesn't! Research shows that giving students control over or choice about what they learn has absolutely no impact on their subsequent results. Interestingly, giving students choices about trivial things (e.g. what colour pen to write in) does have small but positive effect on student outcomes?

Myth: Special Diets Help Behaviour

Reality: Many parents and teachers believe that certain foods lead children to misbehave. One common belief is that sugar leads to hyperactivity and subsequent misbehaviour. Professor Hattie says a review of 16 double-blind, placebo-controlled studies investigating the link between sugar and hyperactivity found that no such link exists. Rather, the misbehaviour of some children can be attributed to parental (or teacher) expectations, the child's expectations (many children have been told that sugar makes them hyperactive), an externalised locus of control and poor parenting. Another common belief is that food additives cause higher levels of hyperactivity in some children. A review of meta-analyses on the topic showed that there is little if any link between food additives and how children behave in the classroom.

Myth: Teachers need to soften criticism with praise

Reality: While giving students positive reinforcement is important, Professor Hattie says coupling critical feedback with praise negates the impact the feedback has on improving student learning. Teachers should work to create a positive, nurturing environment so that students trust their teachers and set high expectations. However, critical feedback should be delivered with a different tone so students understand the importance of improving their work.

Myth: Teachers need deep content knowledge to be effective

Reality: Some reform initiatives focus primarily on ensuring teachers have deeper content knowledge, particularly in secondary subjects. Yet most teaching today occurs at the surface level, so in-depth subject knowledge is not as influential as many believe. It is only when there is the right mix of surface and deep learning does content knowledge matter. Expert teachers use their content knowledge to make meaningful connections between concepts by using students' prior knowledge and adapting lessons to meet students' needs.

Myth: Repeating struggling or immature students accelerates their learning

Reality: Professor Hattie says repeating a grade actually has a negative effect on student achievement (at every age) and is correlated with negative social and emotional adjustment, behaviour and self-concept. Research has shown that struggling students who progress to the next grade often out-perform their peers who have repeated. It should be noted though that academically gifted students who are accelerated forward in a school tend to do well both socially and academically. Research has shown that academically gifted students have more social problems when they are not accelerated.

Myth: Ability grouping is effective

Reality: Professor Hattie says many educators believe grouping students by ability allows teachers to customise learning to students' learning pace. However the opposite is true – it has little impact on achievement. The greatest negative effect is that students from minorities are more likely to be in the lower ability groups and such equity issues should raise major concerns.

ILLUSTRATION 4.3.

(A. Jagan Mohan Reddy,2017)

Charity wrapped in Dignity!!!

She asked him, "How much are you selling the eggs for?"

The old seller replied to her, "Rs.5/(Rupees five)- for one egg, Madam."

She said to him, "I will take 6 eggs for Rs.25/- or I will leave."

The old seller replied, "Come take them at the price you want... May be this is a good beginning because I have not been able sell to anyone today."

She took it and walked away with a feeling that she has won. She got into her fancy car and went to pick her friend, and invited her to a posh restaurant.

She and her friend sat down and ordered what they liked. They ate a little and left a lot of what they ordered.

Then she went to pay the bill. The bill was Rs.1,400/-. She gave him Rs. 1,500/- and said to the owner of the restaurant: "Keep the change."

This incident may seem quite normal to the owner of the restaurant. But it is very painful for the poor egg seller. The bottom line is:

Why do we always show that we have the power when we buy from the needy and the poor? And why are we generous with those who do not need our generosity?

Every time a poor child comes to me to sell something simple, I remember a tweet from the son of a rich man who said, "After every prayer my father used to buy simple goods from poor people at expensive prices, even though he did not need them. Sometimes he used to pay more for them. I used to get concerned by this act and I asked him about it. Then my father told me: "It is a charity wrapped with dignity, my son.

Compare these two stories of social hypocrisy.

The first one is disappointing and the second one is inspiring...!

Illustration: 4.4

The Teacher-Student Relationship in Universities in Jeopardy (Professor Hattie, the Wire)

A university – supposedly a 'temple' of higher learning – cannot escape the ugliness that surrounds our existence. We are a product of the caste prejudices and sexual violence that we, as a part of the intelligentsia, condemn. Stories of victims of caste discrimination and sexual harassment have been surfacing more and more in universities lately. It seems that as teachers, we have lost our moral grounding.

Universities are increasingly becoming a war zone, filled with doubt, grievance committees and surveillance machineries. Even though I know that a university is not a solitary island and that in a caste-ridden and patriarchal society, asymmetrical power relations operate through diverse forms of sadism and exploitation, something keeps haunting me. Is there nothing beautiful and life-sustaining left in the teacher-taught relationship? Is it possible to create a community of learners if we normalise negativity with our harsh realism and refuse to believe that no legal machinery and social media campaigning can replace the power of love, care and trust?

Understanding the 'darkness' surrounding universities

However, before I speak of these 'lost ideals', I wish to understand the darkness surrounding us. To begin with, let me reflect on caste hierarchy and classroom dynamics. The social composition of students in public universities is changing, with students from marginalised castes and communities – many of them first-generation learners – securing admissions. As the university, to use Pierre Bourdieu's words, is inherently inclined to some sort of 'cultural capital', many of them find it difficult to cope with the academic pressure. This gap prevails because of unequal schooling and monopoly of the cultural elite in the transaction of knowledge traditions. Not solely that. They also experience some form of violence – not necessarily always physical, but essentially symbolic and psychic. They realise that their experiences and skills are devalued, and because of a complex process of official as well as social classification, they have already acquired some sort of 'stigmatised' identity. This leads to hypersensitivity: an intense feeling of betrayal, doubt and suspicion. No wonder it is becoming increasingly difficult for them to believe that a teacher from a so-called forward caste can also be their friend and well-wisher.

Moreover, we, as teachers from a privileged background, fail to understand their inner turmoil and psychic struggle. Despite theoretical cognition of 'liberty, equality and fraternity', caste, it seems, lies in the ok deeper layers of our existence. Furthermore, in an over-crowded classroom in which covering the syllabus and conducting exams are the primary tasks, where is the possibility of a delicate and sustained interaction of human souls? Thus, in an emotionally charged environment, suspicion is normalised, everything takes a political turn, and even an unintended mistake by an otherwise well-meaning teacher is turned into a scandal. As politics of doubt become all-pervading, there is no space for patience and forgiveness, for mutual self-improvement and faith. [As reported in The Wire]

ILLUSTRATION: 4.5

(Prof. P. Waghodekar)

The present scenario of the "temple of higher learning" presented is not unrealistic but a ground reality. It does not mean that earlier the scenario was different. What today we see is the extrapolation what we have been doing since last 7 decades. It was not built overnight. Neither I want to finger at any one, nor can I propose some solid proposals. But often untoward cases are capturing headlines, the reasons are:

Anyhow the teachers' philosophy has drastically changed from service to production shops by virtue of the ecological system in the Indian education sector, e.g., when I was in primary school, mid-50s,, teachers used to treat students equal, my teacher, Patil, used to come to my residence early in the morning and took a band of students for running, a football coach used to be always on football ground (not so good) play daily in the evening, etc. No body could think of tuition classes then and we never found that teacher's were discriminating students say on caste, religion, rich-poor, and basis.

The social media now plays a dominant role to bring the breaking news on front.

People are most freedom and Constitution conscious and almost every issue is politicized.

The epicenter has shifted from university to somewhere else.

If a small cluster of agitators can mend the university/regulatory bodies/government, is it really a democratic mode of functioning?

Why education bodies have been failing to take timely action against the non-academic moves in the campuses and control them?

It has been widely accepted let the education (created) issues be resolved by judiciary. Most of the verdicts in the education sector are coming through judiciary.

Only from symptoms to infer that "The Teacher - Student Relationship in Universities in Jeopardy" is not a proper root-cause analysis. To me it is just passing the buck for the ills I have done..

(page purposely kept blank)

Chapter 5. VALUE BASED EDUCATION

Since long time value based education has been part of human life. Value based education is very common and popular phrase among academicians and reformers. Many architect of ancient and contemporary education have advocated about the importance of value based education in the interest of the world's growing population and its future consequences. According to them only "value" has power to save the word from different types of unwanted natural calamities. But the most important thing that needs to be understood are,

Q. What is value based education?

Q. What is value?

Q. What makes it so important?

Q. What are the major components of value based education?

Q. Is it measurable? If Yes, then

Q. How to measure it?

Q. Who will deliver the value?

Q. Is it possible to breed value among people?

Q. Are teachers compatible to breed value among students?

Q. Does parents think to breed the value in their children?

Q. Who would be the best in breeding values, teachers or parents or both?

A large number of questions come into the mind to shake the tree of rooted Education Confinement which is already loaded with number of incomplete assignments and complicated worksheets that has to be solved first. Most of the questions of these assignments and worksheets are contribution to the modern world civilization for which education is just a commercial entity for gaining profit. These people believes in producing "machines" as end product rather than "magnificent mind" to solve the unsolved puzzle of this fast moving world.

Components of Value Based Education

There is no proper and fixed definition in regard to value based education and its components. Several eminent scholars and educationist have defined it in their own ways as per their experience, knowledge and convenience at different interval of time. But most of them tried to consider scenario of their time and expected outcome in future.

Value based education may consist of following vital components,

(i) Ability to understand the basics of humanity and law of nature.

(ii) Ability to differentiate between man, human and inhuman.

(iii) Able to establish the ecological balance through the time, money, resource and space.

(iv) Have respect, honour, affinity and affection for living and non-living.

(v) Should not be judgmental always.

(vi) Must be holistic and optimistic in all types of dealings and approach.

(vii) Good amalgam of love, compassion and renunciation at most.

(viii) Gives importance of dedication, devotion and divinity.

(ix) Be ethical, impartial and improvisate.

(x) Successor of morality.

In general value based education can be decided into two major things that is,

(I) Scientific Value

(II) Morale Value

Whereas scientific value deals with *Logical Framework Approach(LFA)*, there morale value mostly deals with *Holistic Ethical Approach(HEA).* Both are linked with environmental analysis, situational analysis, operational analysis and performance analysis.

The major difference in these two approach is that in case of LFA certain factors may be changed as per time and situation instantly considering its expected impact but in case of HEA, it would be difficult to change the factors immediately even though it required to change as ethics doesn't allow a person to do so. HEA always considers the long lasting impact rather than immediate effect.

Value make people's life simple and sustainable with environment. It brings stability and consistency in life style of human beings. It also helps in transformation, reformation and harmonisation.

Illustration: 5.1

(Lesson from Mahabharatha (Famous Indian Scripture)

One day Krishna & Arjuna were taking their usual walk, when they came across an old Brahmin begging, taking pity on his condition, Arjuna gave him a bag of gold coins.

The man was overjoyed. On his way to home, he was robbed by a thief in the forest. He cursed his fate and the next day set off to beg again.

Arjuna & Krishna saw him again & got to know his story. Arjuna once again took pity and gave him a large diamond.

The man took it home and kept it in an old pot which had been unused for many years inorder to keep it safe and went to sleep.

The next morning before he could wake up, his wife went to fetch water from the river & on her way back, she slipped and her pot broke. She immediately remembered the pot at home which lay unused and brought it to fill it with water. Just as she dipped the pot in to the river the diamond escaped the pot and went in to the river.

When she returned home the Brahmin was desperately searching the house for the pot & when he saw it in his wife's hands, he got to know what had happened. Dejected with what had happened, he once again left to go begging.

Once again Arjuna and Krishna saw him and when Arjuna heard of the unfortunate incident that had happened, he told Krishna,

"I don't think this man is destined to be blessed at all; I don't think I can help him anymore".

Krishna then gave the man two pennies and the man took them and walked away.

Arjuna then asked Krishna," My Lord, if gold coins and diamond could not change his condition, what good can two pennies does to him?"

Krishna smiled and replied, "let us see".

As the man walked home he was cursing his fate when he saw a fish that had just been caught by a fisherman and was struggling for its life, he took pity on it and thought to himself, " these two pennies cannot fetch me food anyway, let me at least save the life of this creature" and he purchased the fish and was about to throw it in the river when he saw that the breathlessness of the fish was caused due to some large obstruction in its mouth and when removed it , it was the very diamond he had lost in the river. He was overjoyed and started shouting "Look what I found! Look what I found".

At this very time the thief that had robbed him in the forest was passing by and heard his shouts, he recognized the man and thought that man too recognized him and was thus shouting. Fearing that the Brahmin may take him to be executed, he rushed to him and begged for his forgiveness and returned all the gold coins he had stolen from him. The Brahmin was happy and walked away joyfully with all his wealth.

He went straight to Arjuna to narrate the turn of events and thanked him for all his help and went away.

Arjuna then asked Krishna,

"My Lord, how is it that my gold and diamond could not help him but your meager two pennies did?

Krishna replied," when he had the gold and diamonds he was only thinking of himself and his needs, but when he had the two pennies he put the needs of another creature before his and so I took care of his needs.

The truth is O Arjuna when you think of the pain and needs of others and work to help them, you are doing God's work and hence God Himself takes care of you".

Illustration: 5.2

GLASS, LAKE, SALT & EMOTIONAL QUOTIENT: AN INSPIRATIONAL STORY

The old Master instructed the unhappy young man to put a handful of salt in a glass of water and then to drink it.

"*How does it taste?*" the Master asked.

"Not good at all," spat the apprentice.

The Master chuckled and then asked the young man to take another handful of salt and put it in the lake. The two walked in silence to the nearby lake and when the apprentice swirled his handful of salt into the lake, the old man said, "Now drink from the lake."

As the water dripped down the young man's chin, the Master asked,

"How does it taste?"

"Good!" remarked the apprentice.

"Do you taste the salt?" asked the Master.

"No," said the young man.

The Master sat beside this troubled young man, took his hands, and said, "*The pain of life is pure salt; no more, no less. The amount of pain in life remains the same, exactly the same. But the amount we taste the 'pain' depends on the container we put it into. So when you are in pain, the only thing that you can do is to enlarge your sense of things.....*

Water is a great teacher that shows us how to move through the world with grace, ease, determination, and humility. The journey of water as it flows upon the earth can be a mirror of our own paths through life. Water begins its residence on earth as it falls from the sky or melts from ice and streams down a mountain into a tributary or stream. In the same way, we come into the world and begin our lives on earth. Like a river that flows within the confines of its banks, we are born with certain defining characteristics that govern our identity. We are born in a specific time and place, within a specific family, and with certain gifts and challenges. Within these parameters, we move through life, encountering many twists, turns, and obstacles along the way just as a river flows. Water is a great teacher that shows us how to move through the world with grace, ease, determination, and humility. When a river breaks at a waterfall, it gains energy and moves on, as we encounter our own waterfalls, we may fall hard but we always keep moving on. Water can inspire us to not become rigid with fear or cling to what's familiar. Water is brave and does not waste time clinging to its past, but flows onward without looking back. At the same time, when there is a hole to be filled, water does not run away from it in fear of the dark; instead, water humbly and bravely fills the empty space. In the same way, we can face the dark moments of our life rather than run away from them. Eventually, a river will empty into the sea. Water does not hold back from joining with a larger body, nor does it fear a loss of identity or control. It gracefully and humbly tumbles into the vastness by contributing its energy and merging without resistance. Each time we move beyond our individual egos to become part of something bigger, we can try our best to follow the lead of the river.

Education and Training In Non - Violence should be Part of the Curriculum ? (P. Waghodekar'2017 MTC).

Time is infinite, immeasurable, in fact, beyond the perception of man, and it is compartmentalized into ages for man's convenience, understanding and analysis. We term them as dark, stone, medieval, modern age, etc. Modern is a relative term, not absolute. I am modern because hopefully I am leading a better quality-life using more advanced resources than those available to my preceding generations. I believe in any age, man uses his wit and wisdom for his survival that has made our existence possible today.

What are the five Yamas (abstinence: self-restraint, self-denial)?

- Non-injury/non violence
- No theft (no stealing)
- No hoarding (non-possession)
- Celibacy (non-indulgence)
- Speak truth (non-false hood)

The world is rolling because these Yamas exist in one or the form without regards to their varying degrees of existing extent but co-existing in any age. The total evolution of man can be achieved by adopting these Values rightly preached by Patanjali, adopted by Jainism and propagated by the great souls like Mahatma Gandhi, and Jesus. Education system is a sub-system of the larger ecological-system the country has adopted. Good and bad attributes of the larger system does appear in her sub-systems.

Wise knows that education is for the ultimate well-fare and well being of the society. It is expected to do good for the present generation and the coming generations too. But the expectation is fulfilled provided.

Illustration: 5.3

(Usha K. Shankar'2017, Tugboat Consulting and Marketing Services LLC)

Good, bad, evil are all learnt from the eco system.Education only adds more value to it .

So if a child grows up hearing about siblings murdering each other and extra marital affairs,if a child sees his mother being beaten,he learns it as HIS way of life. IF the movie posters show the hero in anger, or with a women or with a sword or a gun pointing at my face,a child accepts ALL of it.

I was in school during the hippie invasion-drugs and LSD and music-all surrounded us.I had classmates who drank and took drugs.Yet my mother made it a point to sit us down and show us why a choice of how we live was important and where the paths would lead us.And so one could sway us.

Today it's different; the pressure on the child is just beyond belief. Schools say be honest and ethical-and all it sees around is adults not being so; be good and kind yet all it sees everywhere is violence and death.

Schools or homes dont educate. They preach .

Bandura's Bobo doll experiment is so real today.

What is the way out?

We should not give up. As a professor we all see violence in each and every aspect of our life. It is only our stand and determination that can stop it. A child doesn't have to be taught to pick up a Gun

However If we want him to be soldier of Non Violence it will be easier. Teaching and training in Non violence gives power of communication to students it is not Robotics or Rocket science. It is only a question of our attitudes and mind set.

Illustration: 5.4

(R. Deshpande, 2017)

(Research Fellow, Centre for Gandhian Thoughts and Peace Studies at Central University, India)

When a four-year old is booked for rape, there is not much behind which we can hide,

When a child who is probably still watching Peppa Pig cartoons needs swab tests,

You realize that degeneration of our society is almost complete.

This ghastly incident comes at a time when we are still grappling with the twists in the murder of seven- year-old

Pradyuman Thakur in Ryan International School allegedly murdered by a senior who slit his throat perhaps just to postpone his exams.

As easy as that.Like the mother of the four-year old wrote in her letter, schools are second homes for our children, it is where they spend as much time as they do in their house and where we let them go with full trust.

Yet a little child was left to button up by herself with not one elder in the vicinity while she was assaulted,

that is an age when we dress them up lovingly ourselves. The shame is ours.

How did a young boy behave so debauched?

The above incidents are just a tip of the iceberg of violence in our educational institutions.

Have our educational institutions become powerhouse of money making? Is it not time to look at the basic skills like human relations be taught at schools

Belief in Legacy (History of Eminent Social Reformers, Philosophers, Educationist and Optimist Leaders).

Whatever innovations and innovative things that you see in present are the results of past actions. Even inferences of any research is also based on past, that means only original or transformed form of past exists in the world or inherited for the belief and benefits of future generations which is going to become past.

Present is perishable, it could not be constant.

Therefore we must develop faith/trust in glorious past that is "history" and heritage.

Believe or not, but past will always exist in legacy.

Therefore, whether Mahatma Gandhi, Nelson Mandela or Martin Luther king, belief need to be tested, developed and survived in long term for the sake of humanity and peace.

(Page purposely left blank)

Chapter

6. HOLISTIC EDUCATION

Gandhian thoughts of basic education system and inclusion of hospitality as subject would be of great help in developing and breeding holistic approach of Education in the world.

The world has been moving fast through leaps and bounds leaving the holistic approach of education behind, is the main reason of various global disasters and crisis that this beautiful earth has been facing since we wandered from the main pathway of education. The second important aspect of education is also missing from almost all types of conventional and technical programmes and its structure that is component of "Hospitality" as one subject for making people adaptive and adorable with environment. Emphasizing on breeding reflective (eternal) education rather than prescriptive(list of rules and regulations) education is the main concerned in education. Gandhian thought of basic education system given by Mahatma Gandhi and introducing Hospitality as an important subject in all types of programmes may lead a rigid foundation of holistic education in the world for peaceful life with happiness. And commercialization of education has posed education as luxury product in the world, which is beyond the capacity and reach of poor people.

Since a long time, education has been remained in focus area for the doctrine makers and preachers. Many times it posed many challenges and issues before reformers due to the varying geography and prevailing condition of region. Education is a driving force of world economy that could only help in sustainable development and conservation of scarce resource linked with environment. It has various forms and each form has its own significance and value in terms of human life and dynamic world. Education generates knowledge; thoughts; ideas; skills; kindness and humanity within human being that no one can steal until it is being offered to the seeker. It is like river that originates to serve the world. Commodification and commercialization of education has posed education as luxury product in the world, which is beyond the capacity and reach of poor people. And rising inflation of daily use commodities has added a big barrier of getting it on time. The paper reveals some real facts that are missing from education framework. Education should not be the reason of poverty in the world. And poverty should not be the reason of illiteracy in the world. The purpose of education must be oriented towards generating peace, prosperity, happiness, eligibility and employability with humanity.

It is well said, that if, you educate one man, you educate one man only but if, you educate one woman, you educate whole family.

Learning is Growth and Innovation is Process.

The whole idea of holistic education is based on overall development of human beings rather than one sided development. It is well said that "Man is Producer and Controller of his own situations ". It is misconception that "Man can't change so better to change the situations". Instead of moving towards prescriptive education it's better to adopt reflective education. To understand the difference the following example can be taken,

Suppose two people are there in the world one is very strict in following the rules and regulations for showing the right behaviour to the people. The second who doesn't follow the all rules and regulations but has positive belief for living and non-living both.

Now the key question is,

Who is great?

1. Person predicting right "Behaviour"

2. Person has highly respect, affinity, love and honour for every living and non-living both that is with "Holistic Beliefs".

Behaviour of a person can be seen from eyes so it is tangible in nature. But belief can't be seen with open eyes so it is intangible. Therefore one conclusion can be drawn on the basis of above example that a person who follows strictly rules and regulations with right behavior but eternally (belief) has no honour and respect for living and non living may be good in attracting people for achieving short term goal but in long term he would be Villon for this world. And such types of person are liable for various types of corruption, global crisis, disasters and global warming.

On the other way person having good belief and who thinks for everyone but sometimes breaks the rules and regulations are good in long term for world.

So many great people came and went with holistic education approach but this world failed to adopt their philosophy and approach.

Does education fills or kills?

Most of time more qualified people behave like more irresponsible, irrelevant, and more inhuman. Somewhere holistic approach in education is missing.

What is most important to earn in life as an intellectual?

Options are (i) Brahmagyan (supreme knowledge and wisdom to serve the world) (ii) Brahmastra (Supreme power- a weapon that could destroy the world within seconds) (iii) Draupadi (conflicts, clashes or war).

Many intellectuals have done wonderful tasks and unparalleled inventions in the history of science, social-science and arts. But ultimately what they achieved has been used in the construction or destruction of this world.

Take the following quotation from great Indian Epics/scriptures and try to feel the importance of holistic education in life. The quotation is,

"Guru Govinda Dono Khare, Kaake Lagu Pao !

Balihari Guru Aapno Govinda Diyo Batay.!!"

It was said in above lines that Teacher and God when both have come to your door and standing in front of you then whom should you give honour (hospitality) first? And in answer it was said that, it's better to give honour to your teacher first as he has shown you the path to find the God and treasures of knowledge.

There is an urgent need to develop a new learning curriculum and technology to cover the entire educational spectrum of the country to meet with world spectrum. The continuous research work will find the ways of expanding the education network at regional and central level.

Prayer: Perspective of Education (R. Deshpande, MTC'2017).

A question was posed to Mahatma Gandhi, "You believe in mass prayer. Is congregational worship as practised today, a true prayer?

In my opinion, it is a degrading thing and therefore dangerous.

Jesus said: "When thou prayest, thou shalt not be as the hypocrites are,

but enter into thine inner chamber and having shut thy door pray to the Father which is in secret.

" Most people in a crowd are inattentive and unable to concentrate. Prayer then becomes hypocrisy.

The Yogi is aware of this. Should not the masses, therefore, be taught selfexamination which is the true prayer?

Gandhiji's answer: "I hold that congregational worship held by me, is true prayer for a collection of men.

The convener is a believer and no hypocrite. If he were one, the prayer would be tainted at the source.

The men and women who attend have no contact with the convener. Hence it is presumed; they do not come for show.

They join in because they believe that they somehow or other, acquire merit by having common prayer.

That most or some persons are inattentive or unable to concentrate is very true.

That merely shows that they are beginners. Neither inattention nor inability to concentrate is any proof of hypocrisy or falsity.

It would be, if they pretended to be attentive when they were not.

On the contrary, many have often asked me what they should do, when they are unable to concentrate.

The adage of Jesus quoted in the question, is wholly inapplicable.. Jesus was referring to individual prayer and to hypocrisy underlying it.

There is nothing in the verse quoted, against collective prayer. I have remarked often enough that without individual prayer,

Collective prayer is not of much use. I hold that individual prayer is a prelude to collective, as the latter, when it is effective,

Must lead to the individual. In other words, when a man has up on to the stage of heart prayer, he prays always,

Whether in the secret or in the multitude I do not know what the questioner's Yogi does or does not.

I know that the masses when they are in tune with the Infinite naturally resort to self-examination. All real prayer must have that end.

The arguments for individual prayer and prayer in mass (P. Wakhidekar'2017, MTC).

The arguments for individual prayer and prayer in mass needs further in depth analysis.

Prayer is the only time pr oven tool to become one with the Cosmos, "Aham Brahmsmi".

Prayer is a dialogue between individual's soul and God wherein the individual peeps in deep within, searches for Godly traits, and attains the Godhood.

In mass prayer, many individuals come under the supervision of a convener who may be competent enough or may not be.

In mass prayer the collective (unified) effect can be seen in a limited way in worldly affairs not necessarily in spiritual domain. Thus, it depends upon the type of individuals and their motives who have assembled over there.

Like Mass yoga postures, mass prayer can improve the public awareness but man's total evolution does not take place (Kuldeep Nagi, 2017, MTC Global).

The human beings have invented many sophisticated means, methods, rites, and ritual to become one with God. It's not sure what fauna and flora on this planet will have to do? Most animals gaze at the sky and walk on earth and wonder about their existence. They seem to be already aligned with the power of nature and God without prayers and all jingle bells. In other words, the evolution of intelligence has its own consequences, insecurity is one of them.

It seems like each religion has created an environment (some call it spirituality, divinity, and all that) that is itself is inherently regarded as corrupt and degrading. Prayers can help when it is aligned with the inner self. There is nothing out there except the infinite Cosmo and things beyond, not even oxygen and alien life. Let us pray the God for a better understanding of our existence on this planet. And do keep in mind the plight of fauna and flora that keeps us alive.

Prayers when made go up (upload) in the cosmos or universe and network is caught with Supreme power and whatever is wanted or desired becomes reality (download) in life of the person who prays (P.K.Keshap, 2017, MTC global).

Yes, it may take a day, a month, a year, a decade, couple of decade and sometimes many decades. In my case, it has taken many decades but the wish or my dream is fulfilled at the age of 60. So, I love praying.

When I pray and the prayers are not fulfilled, I just look at my mobile phone.

When I travel, many railway stations pass and the mobile does not catch the network. But thereafter it catches and works well.

Same feelings I have when my prayers are not responded. I feel when mobile network was not caught; I did not throw my mobile phone but kept on waiting for the network.

Why should I stop praying if my wishes are not fulfilled instantly or for some time?

(page purposely kept blank)

7. EDUCATION SYSTEM IN THE WORLD

System is important for distribution of education under a proper framework. It minimizes the chances of disparity and facilitates a smooth learning oriented mechanism of delivery. In general there are three types of system which is very common in the world. One is government system, second is private system and third is public-private partnership. Each system has its own draw back. Blaming each other for incomplete tasks and imposing allegation is normal these days.

Q. Who has been becoming the main victim?

Victims are those student (learner) and teacher who are free from any political instigations thinking only for his career and holistic growth of nations and world as well.

Politics has entered into the education system like big monster. And it is said "politics is a dirty game". Politics has polluted the sacred Ganga (a holy river) of education. It's not allowing the fishes to come out without getting untouched. Promoting student unions representing various political parties in colleges and universities have spoiled the whole system of education and its delivery mechanisms that need to be stopped immediately. Education must be free from all types of biased and cruel thoughts.

Latest technology has given new dimensions to the education system by making it easy to access from far most corners. But it has several draw back that need to be carefully checked and removed. Technology has brought both learners and teachers closer to each other to ensure the delivery and facilitating the understanding. It has been helping in various areas including of medical treatment and engineering.

System has its own draw back but generally holistic education system would be the right way to satisfy the need of learner, teacher and environment in sustainable way. System must be simple, flexible and open to accept the practical experiences and adaptive in nature. It must provide opportunities to learn for various types of learner keeping aside caste, culture, class, sex, age, income and inequalities. It should open the door for both regular and working class learners without comparing the distant and unruly eligibility conditions.

Q. Do grades still matter anymore?

Several studies have shown that performance at school, as measured by grades and scores on standardized tests, does not correlate with success after graduation. "IQ offers little to explain the different destinies of people with roughly equal promises, schooling, and opportunity," Daniel Goleman writes in his best-seller, Emotional Intelligence.

"When 95 Harvard students from the classes of the 1940s were followed into middle age, the men with the highest test scores in college were not particularly successful compared to their lower-scoring peers in terms of salary, productivity or status in their field, nor did they have the greatest life satisfaction, nor the most happiness with friendships, family and romantic relationships."

And with the rise of artificial intelligence and machine learning, the skills that students need to learn to find a job and be successful is changing fast. In a recent Harvard Business Review article, Ed Hess, a professor at the University of Virginia's Darden Graduate School of Business, argues that in the AI age, our definition of "smart" will be completely transformed. Since we won't have much of a chance against supercomputers that can calculate far faster than our brains could possibly, we'll need to rely on completely different ways for humans to add value.

"The new smart will be determined not by what or how you know but by the quality of your thinking, listening, relating, collaborating, and learning. Quantity is replaced by quality. And that shift will enable us to focus on the hard work of taking our cognitive and emotional skills to a much higher level," Hess argues.

If robots and artificial intelligence are going to change how we work and the skills that we'll need to do our jobs-- whatever those jobs might look like in the future--are grades earned in college or graduate school an adequate indicator of the potential to succeed?

Q. Can teachers fix the education system?

Educational system can be influenced by observable teacher actions that have an impact on students; the associated vital aspects about accomplished teacher may include following:

Knowledge of Students: students have of themselves and of their career choices.

Knowledge of Content: body of knowledge related to an appreciation of technical, cross-disciplinary, and transferable skills and concepts.

Learning Environments and Instructional Practices: the pedagogical dynamics.

Career Progression: to address the pursuit of both educational and professional opportunities.

- Program Design and Management.
- Partnerships and Collaborations.
- Leadership in the Profession.
- Reflective Practice.

Infact only teacher can change.

Think of great teachers of society- Swami Vivekananda, Gautama Buddha

Think of top institutions across globe and field of studies, its teachers who are central and bring results.

Think of super30 and likes,

Can we think of education system without teacher, no, since teacher is core aspect to education ecosystem and core can only change?

Teachers are the only resource to effect any change in the education system and attempt to fix it. For this only those teachers who have the requisite skills and willingness to learn and aptitude for self development would be able to make an impact.

Teachers with long years of teaching experience are not necessarily equipped to make any systemic change or 'fix' the system, as they live by the system that they have mastered.

We are still complaining of NCERT books being below standards, coming with spelling errors etc. How can we ever let that command what our kids should learn. Can we trust this dated knowledge? Rather schools and teachers who adopt and strictly follow a dynamic system of curriculum management are the only institutions who know what is to be done and how to do it. FIX the system. Besides, if they are not tech savvy, no one believes and trusts what they can do or have done.

Let's do a poll and check from the group how many members' children go to schools with flexible and dynamic curriculum systems or is anyone aware of any such school in India.

Let's review this and then ask to FIXING it with a viable solution and not with old a conventional approach which has not delivered up to expectations. I do mean to keep aside the small token percentage of successful Indian and worried about the rest 90+% of population. The boards are doing their bit in restricting change and damaging the system further. Members may already be aware of the same.

Yes, Teachers are the only resource and they have to be empowered to fix the system as a 'continuous process'

Teacher is not the sage on the stage (Bholanath Dutta'2017, MTC Global) but should be coach by the sides of the students. This can be achieved when we shift the focus from content master to learning master. Technology can be a great enabler. Big dream does not need big budget.

Teacher is not the sage on the stage but should be coach by the sides of the students: Teacher who uses experiential teaching-learning process is by nature a coach himself/herself, student centered and always found by the sides of students.

This can be achieved when we shift the focus from content master to learning master (Prabhakar Waghodekar'2017 MTC Global): Content master simply omits, reproduces contents not necessarily always in a meaningful way, in a lively manner, whereas learning master kindles the quest from within of individual student to learn something more and more as learning is an individual's spontaneous waking up from within, unstoppable.

Technology can be a great enabler. It remains so always. But proves to be of no value if, used as an animate skeleton/gadget/ritual. It cannot be the soul of any activity anytime, however.

Big dream does not need big budget. It is true. Nevertheless, big dream cannot fetch outcome unless it is not backed by untiring efforts, determination, as a mission in fact.

Nothing has been failed in Education. Education is divine by nature. Only we are failed to understand it. Education always gives impact through its multidimensional effects (negative or positive). The main obstacle is human being itself who possess "comparative nature" with everlasting ego. Making differentiation/comparison is also nature of human by virtue.

Q. Why to run behind getting A, B, C, D?

Q. Why do we need a world ranking?

Q. Is legacy of any country depends on world ranking?

Q. Does world ranking of any institutions really matters to produce craftsmen of future or present or holistic intellectuals?

Q. Does education require a ranking or grading?

Education would be unmatched, unparalleled and indemnified in any part of the world till it retains the nature of divinity and carries essence of sustainability, holistic viability and humus of credibility.

Degree/Certificate is just a non-living paper without education (divine/holistic/sustainable).
Mushrooming like private institutions are the main actors and culprits that need to be focused on. Poverty and location should not be the barriers of Education. Expensive Education is curse that needs to be stopped immediately.

Education is Ganga, Stop polluting it.

How to take the Ganga of Education to the door step of remotest child? That should be the only aim and objective of educationist / intellectuals.

Dynamism is good but not by killing divinity.

Along with sound foundation of knowledge, skill, dedication a teacher, a mentor (and any leader) should have

* 360* eye sight to see positive of anything before negative

* Helping hands

* Clear mind

* Clean heart

* Genuine and selfless concern about students, colleagues and all

* Mother's heart to forgive the student

* Quest for quality

* Crystal clear behavior

A teacher should be always devoted to develop his student that he become better and advance version of the teacher himself.

Illustrations:7.1

(Swami Nanda)

Inspiring personality and motivational skills that reflect the impact on the students and their lives over a period of life. The students who were taught in 1998 were asked to give feedback in 2016. Most of them reported upward trend in their lives.

Teacher's traits are fine. I feel they are the input. What about the output?

Feedback as a teacher too matters a lot. This boosts the morale of a teacher too.

For example: A student after 7 years of learning said: Sir, for me, your course is worth 1 crore. Because I got a job in bank and will work there for about 35 years and in 35 years I will earn over 1 crore.

Second student after 3 years said: What I could not learn in 15 days of school and college, that I learnt from you and am M.A (English) now.

He further states: Education is manifestation of qualities already inherent in a student. So, a teacher's job is to facilitate so that the student may exhibit those qualities for the benefit of society, nation, and world, family and self.

Personal traits good but what those personal traits give to the society is also important. Yes they are the inputs that will give above output.

We need to contemplate further on two word "ideal" and "perfection".

To me ideal is optimal or benchmark but perfection is neither equivalent to the best nor to a goal post because perfection is an abstract idea (concept) beyond perception, undefined in real sense like infinity.

No doubt some traits/values can be identified that lead to ideal state or state of perfection but such traits/values are often interwoven and cannot be always identified (measured) in isolation, e.g., sense of belonging is an assemblage of such traits/values as character, loyalty, integrity, honesty, etc.

Finland is ranked one in education practices internationally. The reasons are:

1. Finland system is close to natural process of learning.
2. All stake holders are greatly concerned, involved and supportive.

Gurukul system is also a proven system based on:

1. Duty
2. Spirituality
3. Renunciation
4. Service to Humanity/God
5. No teaching but learning through real-life experiences, examples, queries, discussion, etc.
6. To one according to one's need and potential.

7. .Gurukuls away from cities, .students stay with Guru's family and Eco-friendly.

8. Guru has the highest status in society, even more than the king.

9. Guru totally autonomous and has developed his/her faculties in certain disciplines.

10. Living and tuition free.

11. No caste bar, only requirement is Jidnyasu students: eager to learn!

Ancient rishis had developed 16 Samskaras, thoughtful, scientific and Eco-friendly.

For example, division of life into four Ashramas: Brahmacharyashrama, Grihasthashrama, Vanaprasthashrama and Sansyasashrama. Brahmacharyashram studentship- is the foundation leading to human quality/purposeful life. Depending on the Varnas, Mounj or Upanayana Samskara is done during the age 4 to 6 or 8 years, students used to select his/her Guru in consultation with parents or wise persons and and if found suitable by Guru used to get admitted. The education goes one Tap, twelve years; and by the age 18, the disciple is permitted to enter into Grihasthashrama with Guru's advice: be a good citizen, speak truth and good and act piously. Gurudakshina is given to Guru or as and when later demanded by Guru (P. Waghodekar'2017).

What are the outcomes of such a system, a few examples but to quote:

1. A son of fisherman Valmiki wrote Ramayana.

2. A son of Mehtar- Vyas wrote Mahabharata.

3. Dronacharya turned Arjuna the best warrior and dancer, and Bhima the best cook and wrestler.

4. Arya Chankya turned Chandragupta Mourya a great emperor.

5. Jijamata turned Shivaji into the great General, Social Reformer and Statesman.

6. A son of common man became Adi-Shankarachrya,

7. Ramkrishna pramhansa turned Swami Vivekananda.

The world needs further research in the Gurukul system: especially in such areas as Mounja Samskara, education technology, real-life cases/field examples. support system, etc.

1. No system based on thoughts dies as thought never dies. The ignorance of people makes it to die.

2. Gurukul System is not extinct, not dead, it still being used in different countries especially those following Hindu, Buddha, Jain, Sikh, and Muslim religions. What is about Madarsa and Gurukuls run by different sects in India? Arya Samajist in some Districts in Maharashtra like Latur, Omanabad and Beed and in UP to follow Gurukul System. Dr. Y A Kawade, the founder and mentor of the Gramoudyogik Shikshan Mandal, Aurangabad (Maharashtra), India, is the very outcome of the Arya Samaj Gurukul System. Swami Ramananda Teerth Saraswati, a Sanyasi, who was instrumental for Nizam State of Hyderabad's merger in India in September 1949, is also an outcome of Gurukul Arya Samaj system. Swami Vivekananda and

Adi-Shankaracharya are another two glaring examples, outcomes of Gurukul system. World wide spread of Yoga and of some Hindu Sects is nothing but the outcome of Gurukul system.

3. Finland is a great country, achieved world top position in 'real' education. Finland education model is approaching the Gurukul model that what I think,and lo! It is based, I fully commit, on experimental evolution, research and research that India has been missing miserably. I have suggested a few areas, within my limited knowledge, for research in Gurukul system.

4. The advanced countries are not understanding the (the invisible thick bondage between Indian parents and kids (irrespective of religions) , among family members and between teacher and taught. India knowingly or unknowingly has been following a culture that preaches " Matru Deo Bhava, Pitru Deo Bhava and Acahrya Deo Bhava" (Mother, Father and Teacher are God to me!).

5. Those countries that forget their past have a little chance to grow in future.

6. But only singing the past glory alone does not take one to one's destination. Efforts, research, quest for excellence, experimentation, determination, etc. are required to be adhered to.

LIBRARY

The role of library in education can't be ignored as it has been remained the back bone of any educational institutions in the world whether it was ancient world famous Nalanda University in India or modern Oxford or Howard University. The format of library has been in the centre of educational institutions and education reformists as it signifies the willingness of research and development approach of any school or university. A resourceful library with all types of modern technology and facilities is also the demand of modern or contemporary education. Digitalisation of library has given the new dimensions to Library Management Information System (LMIS) and internet has added easy to access data approach for information seekers. The following illustration tried to highlight the "the place of university library in degree completion.

ILLUSTRATION: 7.2

Libraries have long counted up the books on their shelves to show their value. That meant Harvard University's library (with 18.9-million books) was clearly superior to Duke University's (with 6.1-million volumes) or University of California at Riverside's (with a mere 3 million titles).

These days, though, libraries are finding new ways to measure their worth. They're counting how many times students use electronic library resources or visit in person, and comparing that to how well the students do in their classes and how likely they are to stay in school and earn a degree. And many library leaders are finding a strong correlation, meaning that students who consume more library materials tend to be more successful academically.

"University libraries have to explain their place in the world of degree completion," says Alan Bearman, dean of university libraries and the Center for Student Success and Retention at Washburn University. "As we all know, there's this big push in the nation about on-time degree completion, and libraries are trying to see where they fit in that world."

These new measures aren't just about bragging rights. Many college leaders now see encouraging library use as a way to boost student success.

Washburn University has been leading that charge. For the last six years, it has made the library a key partner in its student-success drive. Officials started carefully tracking how library use compares to other metrics, and it has made changes as a result—like moving the tutoring center and the writing lab into the library. Those moves were designed not only to lure more people into the stacks, but to make seeking help more socially-acceptable for students who might have been hesitant.

"We've destigmatized getting academic assistance," says Bearman. "They can say, 'I'm going to the library'" instead of having to announce that they're going for tutoring.

When the writing lab was in a different building last year, about 25 students a month came in. Now that the lab is in the library, about 400 to 450 students per month make use of it.

Because Washburn is a largely commuter campus, officials hope that encouraging students to come to the library will increase the time they spend on homework and studying. And Bearman says he replaced cramped worktables and study carrels with larger furniture to keep students there.

"We know if a commuter student leaves campus, life just gets busy," says Bearman. "Now they can spread out and stay longer, and as they stay longer the retention rate went up." Visits to the library have shot up from 108,000 in 2008 to 280,000 last year.

Meanwhile, the retention rate at the university has risen 12 percentage points in the six years since officials started the library reforms. "That's a massive increase at an open-admissions university," says Bearman.

Of course, there's no way to know whether the library visits are causing the improved retention on campus—as researchers like to remind us, correlation does not equal causation. Still, something is working for students, and officials plan to keep watching the data and making design tweaks. And many other libraries are conducting similar experiments with library data (one influential one was done by Adam Murray, dean of libraries and educational technologies at James Madison University.)

Increased Monitoring

Perhaps the biggest change for libraries is creating systems to make library-use data part of the dashboard of options available to administrators across campus.

At Mercer University, for instance, that has meant a partnership between the library, which knows what electronic materials students use, and the technology office, which manages other campus data such as usage of the course-management system. The university is doing a study to see whether library usage there also equates to student success.

Scott Gillies, associate dean of university library at Mercer University, says that having the data at the ready has come in handy when explaining the library's value on campus. One faculty member, for instance, asked why the library invests so much in online materials when the faculty member preferred print. Gillies was able to show with data that online resources were more popular with students, and heavily used.

He hopes that with the data from their study, "we could be more justified in spending money on electronic resources, and we can be more comfortable with them," he says. "And maybe it will help us identify areas where we're under-serving students."

Librarians working on such efforts say they are careful to protect the privacy of individual students, by stripping out names and only reporting aggregate usage information. "We don't care what they're looking up," he says, "we just care that they're looking at resources."

Bearman says his library has also had discussions about protecting student privacy. "We are not tracking what they read," he said, meaning they don't try to isolate which particular article was chosen. "We're not tracking what they search for. We've got a pretty clear line there that we won't cross."

The issue of privacy also emerged during a session on libraries and data at the annual Educause conference earlier this month.

"How much library data do we want to be part of the student learning record?" asked Shane Nackerud, the technology lead on a library-data initiative at the University of Minnesota. "Do we want faculty to be able to see how much library use students have? They could possibly use it to negatively profile students if they don't have high library usage."

He and other library leaders, however, say that it is important for the library to "have a seat at the learning analytics table" to help resolve just that kind of question.

"The library is more than just a repository of stuff," says Bearman, of Washburn University. "It's really central to the student-learning experience. There's a lot of people out there starting to quantify it" (Source: EdSurge).

ILLUSTRATION: 7.3 Case Study

Cellphones Get A Ringing Endorsement In Classrooms (Noelle McGee' 2017):

When Danville High School health teacher Tyler Arnholt gives a lecture, he'll occasionally see a student with his head bent down and one or both hands hidden in his lap, a pocket or a strategically-placed backpack.

To Arnholt, that body language is a tell-tale sign the student is texting, tweeting or messaging on Snapchat.

While the teen may think he's being discreet, "he's not," said Arnholt, who's in his sixth year of teaching.

Arnholt admitted that getting teenagers to put away their personal cellphones can be somewhat of a struggle, mostly at the start of the school year. Still, he doesn't see a need to ban the devices in school.

"I think there's a time for them and a time to put them away," he said, adding the technology can be used as an educational tool. "I don't mind when their phones are out if they're taking notes or looking up something we're talking about in class.

"But if I see they're abusing that privilege — going on Snapchat or Instagram — I don't mind taking that privilege away. And if it gets to be a problem, I don't mind having a one-on-one conversation with that student about respecting how and when they can use it."

When students started bringing mobile phones, MP3 players, tablets and other personal electronic devices to school, districts implemented strict policies to prevent incidents such as cheating, taking unauthorized photos and videos, cyberbullying and sexting, as well as distracting them and others from their studies.

Most policies allowed students to bring their phones to school, so that parents could arrange pick-up times with them and reach them in case of emergencies.

However, students had to keep the devices turned off and in their locker or bookbag. They could only use them after school or in emergency situations approved by a teacher or administrator.

• • • • •

That's still the rule at elementary schools and most middle and junior high schools.

But in recent years, a number of area districts have relaxed the rules for high school students.

For example, high school students in Bement, Champaign, Heritage, Monticello, Oakwood, Salt Fork and Urbana can use their phones in the hallways during passing periods and in the commons during lunch.

While powering on during passing periods is prohibited at St. Joseph-Ogden High School, students have an open campus lunch policy, and many of them use that time to scroll through their news feeds and connect with friends off campus or in the cafeteria.

While most policies still state that phones are forbidden in the classroom, many administrators give teachers the ability to use them at their discretion.

"Technology isn't going to go away," said Monticello Principal Adam Clapp, who estimates that 80 to 90 percent of his school's 534 students carry some type of phone, if not a smartphone. "So, we want to embrace it and take advantage of it for educational purposes."

Other educators share that feeling.

"As it advances, we have to adjust our teaching to reflect the society we live in," said Salt Fork Principal Darin Chambliss, a longtime proponent of smart integration of technology in the classroom.

"Back in the day, we had loose-leaf notebooks. Now students take notes on their smartphone," he continued, pointing out the devices — basically compact computers — have replaced watches and calendars, calculators and dictionaries, encyclopedias and other tools.

"I've known students who've written papers on their smartphones," added Tim Lee, Oakwood High School's principal. "They're thumb-typers, but they're fast."

The administrators pointed out their students will soon be going on to college and careers, where they'll be expected to know how to use technology.

"We need to change the culture ... and teach them about smart integration of technology and how to use it appropriately and responsibly," Chambliss said.

• • • • •

Educators acknowledged that giving students more latitude with their phones can be a slippery slope. While using their phone's calculator or going to Google Docs, students might update their Facebook status or check out their friends' Instagram posts.

But since modifying their policies, educators reported a decrease in incidents of misuse.

"I had my doubts when we started to relax the usage, but the students have handled it very well, and incidents with electronics are much lower than I ever expected," said Tom Davis, superintendent of Heritage schools.

Last year, Salt Fork had only 20 referrals and St. Joseph-Ogden High School had only 15, according Chambliss and SJ-O Principal Gary Page.

"We don't have a lot of discipline problems" in general, Page said. As for cellphones, "we opened it up last year on a trial basis. We said if we start seeing issues with social media and bullying, we'll shut it down, but we haven't. For the most part, our students have used them responsibly. We want to reward that."

Georgetown-Ridge Farm High School Principal Kevin Thomas said incidents there, where phones must be kept off and out of sight unless OK'd by teachers, were cut in half.

Bement High had "maybe a dozen" incidents last year, according to Principal Doug Kepley.

"They've really diminished over the last couple of years," he said. "Students know they're going to have that time to check ... and stay connected throughout the day, maybe even check in with family. And by not having them in the classroom during instruction time, it doesn't hinder what the teachers want to accomplish during class."

• • • • •

Urbana High, which has an enrollment of 1,200, went from 451 cellphone referrals in 2015-16 to 278 last year, said Assistant Principal Erin Ludwick. The vast majority involved kids going onto social networking sites.

While Ludwick is pleased that incidents are down — a trend in all discipline cases, she noted — it's still an issue.

"Last year, cellphone referrals were the No. 1 referral (for discipline problems). We're not happy about that," she said, adding she's at least relieved it's a passive behavior that doesn't cause too much disruption of the learning environment.

Violators are given a verbal warning for the first offense. They can see the dean and be given a lunch detention or made to attend Saturday school for subsequent offenses.

"We strive to use consequences that do not remove them from the classroom environment," Ludwick said, adding chronic offenders can be suspended for insubordination but "we usually don't get there."

Ludwick said officials are continuing to address the issue on the front end. Based on a needs assessment of staff from last year, the Positive Behavioral Intervention and Supports team developed a cellphone etiquette lesson that teachers will cover during a homeroom class this month.

"They'll go over Urbana High School's policy, and there will be some discussion questions: Should people be able to use cellphones anywhere they want, should you use your cellphone in certain social situations, should they be banned in certain places?" Ludwick said, adding the information will be used to put more interventions in place.

Other districts also have teachers or other staff go over electronic device rules, including cyberbullying and sexting, with students and even parents.

Champaign County Sheriff's Deputy Kevin Franzen, the school resource officer for Heritage and Unity schools, recently did that at Parent University in Homer, Davis said.

• • • • •

Meanwhile, administrators said teachers are doing a good job of balancing tech and the curriculum they're charged with teaching.

At Urbana High, some teachers have battery-charging stations that students can plug their phones into while focusing on their lesson, Ludwick said.

"Kids never want their battery to die," she said with a laugh.

She said math teacher Dan Bechtel created a "treasure chest" with numbered slots. At the start of the hour, students place their phones in a slot and get a calculator with a correlating number. Bechtel locks the chest during class.

"He would tell you the time it takes at the beginning and end of class is 100 percent worth the uninterrupted intellectual time he has in between," Ludwick said.

One of his colleagues, Amanda Perez-Rosser, encourages her students to turn on their Pocket Points app when she doesn't want them to use their phone in class.

"It's an incentive to lock up their phone," explained the family and consumer sciences teacher. "They get a point every 20 minutes they don't use it. Kids can redeem the points at restaurants like Meatheads and Chili's. They can get a large pizza with one topping at Papa Murphy's."

"I approach it with a policy of respect and create an ownership by the entire class. If assignments aren't being completed or scores start to lower, I take a strict no cellphone policy based on that class and hour," said Salt Fork High School teacher Andrew Johnson, who likes the freedom he's given to decide when students can or can't have them out.

• • • • •

Perez-Rosser and others said they're also taking advantage of the technology to support instruction, whether that's asking students to do research online, writing and editing in Google Docs, reminding them to do their homework in Google Classroom or reviewing material and testing their knowledge on it using the Kahoot! app.

"With Kahoot!, their phone becomes a clicker," said Christopher Barth, who teaches consumer economics, American government and sociology at Georgetown-Ridge Farm. "I can go online and search for a quiz on the material we're studying.

"Students answer the questions independently using their phones, and their answers pop up on my projector," he said. Only the teacher knows how an individual student answered. "That helps me know whether I need to reteach the material to the class or an individual student."

While schools have more Chromebooks, MacBooks, iPads and other electronic devices at their disposal, most don't have one-to-one computers, teachers said. And sometimes, the systems crash.

"If some computers aren't working," said Salt Fork history teacher Phil Surprenant, "students can use their phones to access Google Classroom to complete homework, access notes, write papers, complete discussion posts or anything else they would need to do in my class. Essentially, everything they need for my social studies classes is in the palm of their hand."

Arnholt has allowed students to use their phones to take notes, write papers and do things like track their health on fitness and nutrition apps.

"It's knowledge that they can take with them to college and use throughout their life," said Arnholt, who believes the good outweighs the bad.

"The important thing is to set your expectations and follow through with them," he said, adding all Danville teachers outline their classroom policy in their syllabus. "When you do that, it becomes a non-issue."

(page purposely kept blank)

Chapter 8. SUSTAINABLE EDUCATION

Education must be futuristic in goal, optimistic in thought and deliverable in local context and settings. There is no short cut in education. It has ability to see and understand the truth about people or situations. Present is perishable that keeps on changing every second, minute and hour. Whatever innovations and innovative things that you see in present are the results of past actions. Even inferences of any research is also based on past, that means only original or transformed form of past exists in the world or inherited for the belief and benefits of future generations which is going to become past.

Present is perishable, it could not be constant. Therefore we must develop faith/trust in glorious past that is "history" and heritage.

Believe or not, but past will always exist in legacy.

But again past, present and perhaps, the future, also have a local context. It is sad but true that no one can exactly predict the future based on the past. The present is what matters. That is the law of nature.

Therefore education must be flexible enough to sustain the words of the world.

Education must be interpretative in approach and must meet with the requirement of society and ecology.

Foundation of any education should be based on truth and nonviolence, humanity, and nature conservation.

The best example of sustainable education can be cited from the old days. In earlier days (just 03-04 decades ago) during schooling people use to donate their old books to needy students or even to close relatives or friends. This way they were not only helping the needy people but also contributing to nature conservation and sustainable development.

And even today it is being practiced by some families .Books would always be remained the best friend of students and teachers. It doesn't require artificial power (electricity) to turn its pages. It doesn't work on internet connection. So once you have books it would be remained with you till the last moment of your life provided this you show interest, passion and care for it. And if you want to donate it, just extend your hand to offer it to others at free of cost by saving environment and nature. Once printed, utilize it multiple times without electricity / internet connection (polluting environment). It never got interrupted due to shortage of power bank or failures of connection. It makes your life more easy and eco-friendly. So choice is yours.

On the other hand just follow your teacher to become your mentor. You would be more innovative bubbling with ideas.

Parents and teachers must breed this culture among their ward and students. Schools and colleges must also develop this culture of donating books. Syllabus never changes completely at one instant. So no excuse please. Instead follow the culture of save books please.

It can be said at this point of time that" *gone are the days of books, now it's era of e-books and digital media technology".*

In hearing it sounds great but in reality it has been killing the innovation and conceptualizing ability of one person. At the same time it hurts and damages the nervous system of people which leads to various types of diseases. It makes people lazy and immovable. Advancement of technology has developed tendency of *"short-cuts"* among present generation which further creates stress (tensions) - one of the main reason behind suicide attempt, vulnerability, school disasters, killings and many more unexpected expected.

No doubt that advancement in technology has given a varying degrees of freedom and dimensions to judge and evaluate the things quickly within fraction of second but at the same time has posed some serious incurable challenges before developers (technocrats). And it can't be ignored simply.

Modernization of education (techno savvy or smart education) must go on in line with traditional *"old is gold"* system of holistic education (innovative education/green education).

The purpose of education is not to take the life but to save the life and love the life.

Connecting students with nature; bringing them into nature; teaching them into nature; breeding respect for nature; encouraging them for taking challenges to save nature; developing spirit of humanity and kindness; and imparting lessons of green globe technology would be the real contribution towards sustainable education.

Open education system would be the future of sustainable education. Educationist need to be more focused on open education system that provides diversified opportunities to both learners and teachers to mingle with the natural surroundings in a practicably environment.

More freedom needs to be given to the learners to explore the real life situations in real natural settings at local level.

Sustainable Education Never Allows People to be sat ideally.

Two years ago all world leaders, including Prime Minister Modi, agreed two major accords. They took the details back to their countries for their legislature to read and to agree implementation. Most leaders reconvened, signed the accords, and thus ratified their acceptance of the targets.

One accord is the 2015 UNFCCC Paris Agreement on Climate Change which extends the 1997 Kyoto Protocols coming into force in November 2016. It asks each nation to limit their pollution and so restrict global warming to 1.5 degrees Celsius or less.

The second accord builds upon the 2000 Millennium Goals which had targets to be met in 2015. The new agreement was agreed and ratified by the UN's 70th general assembly in New York (September 2015) and is known as the UN Sustainable Development Goals (SDGs) with 17 main goals to be met by 2030. One goal is to offer universal gender-free education to all children to fully develop their potential. SDGs provide clear guidelines and targets for all countries to adopt in accordance with their own priorities and within global environmental challenges.

In a world increasingly fractious, even chaotic and dangerous, these two accords carry onerous decision-making choices for every nation as major policy changes imply considerable costs at a time when all nations suffer from slow global economic growth. The Swiss banker, UBS, notes many of the wealthy are willing to invest in their new SDG fund which they consider needs about $5 trillion per year worldwide to meet the UN's targets by 2030. The banker believes there is $250 trillion of global private wealth and will set out rules for its investment that benefits all actors in ways in which national governments cannot: this fund might ease governments' difficulties in meeting their SDG targets, especially ones that develop their education systems.

The annual Edelman 'Global Trust Barometer' data shows trust in institutions and governments has plummeted to new lows. Many people question why populism has grown worldwide and why national leaders tend to succumb to populist demands? Their answers are mixed, but they consider better education is the foremost global imperative developing analytical and critical thinking - noting the time from primary school to adult involvement is at least 16 years. The poorly educated ask "so what?" magnifying this into a Twitter storm "we believe social media - they can't be wrong."

Sadly many governments have decimated their previous education budgets as they are 'soft' targets. In India, surveys show that teachers often do not show up for work, creating problems later: 14 per cent of Indian students (when leaving school) cannot read anything, and nearly half school leavers cannot read text meant for 7-year old children. A 2016 study by the Indian Associated Chambers of Commerce and Industry found that only 7 per cent of Business School graduates were worth a job. Nor were engineering graduates any different: about 600,000 engineers graduate in India every year and of those, only 18 per cent were employable.

Achieving good education is not only an issue in India - in the UK (supposedly with a good education system) the British Nutrition Foundation surveying knowledge about healthy eating found nearly a third of five to seven-year-olds thought that cheese came from a plant; that animals are the source of pasta; and fish fingers are made from chicken. And according to PISA, the international comparison of educational achievement, children in the US fare poorly against the best - in Singapore, Japan, Estonia and Canada.

Q. What is education doing for all these people?

Q. Where is their critical thinking ability?

India has the largest global diaspora and many of its brightest are heads of multinational firms registered in the US and elsewhere: by 2012, 16 per cent of start-ups in Silicon Valley had an Indian co-founder even though Indians represented just 6 per cent of California's population. And in India itself there are pockets of brilliance with family-run business taking the lead. The Fortune 500 lists a range of foremost Indian firms located across all economic sectors and across many states: one cannot say that India lacks intelligent children, only that it does not do enough for its masses.

Indian Prime Minister 'Narendra Modi' launched 'Swayam', a MOOC (Massive Open Online Courses) attempting to lift all education achievement, but these self-motivated modules demand the student can read. Prime Minister's Modi's education reforms are a good start and the reform process should be implemented evenly and quickly throughout all States. Mr Modi notes good school access has been achieved, and has directed reforms to ensure good teaching embraces achievable learning goals.

At the Horasis India Meeting in Switzerland delegates suggested more should be done for rural India, not only to decrease wasteful food losses by re-engineering the supply chains, but also to retain the rural population in place instead of letting it flee to crowded towns in search of work. They suggest increasing food processing at source - with cleaning, trimming and packaging absorbing labour. This change implies processing firms take on the necessary apprenticeship education to train poorly educated school leavers. Firms may say they are not in business to educate - but Mr Modi has seen first-hand how such schemes have benefited Swiss firms whose engineering products are second to none and in high demand globally.

Perhaps the most calming route forward is to remove the fear of losing one's job which can be done by giving every adult a universal basic income (UBI). Finland is already making experiments with this concept and India proclaimed in its January 2017 Annual Economic Survey that "it is an interesting idea whose time may be ripe". Such a change by government might increase trust in our institutions and so develop a better environment allowing time for children's education to be redeveloped, and empower apprentice schemes to educate older workers. Better education will enable all people to critically consider alternatives and their consequences rather than following populist herd opinions.

Frank-Jurgen Richter is founder and chairman of Horasis, a global visions community. Horasis hosts the annual Horasis India Meeting (Source: Business Today).

Finland has one of the highest per capita incomes and a relatively small population. India has a per capita income which is at best 5% of the Finland level. The population in India is about 80 times in excess.

What are we comparing?

Very sensible to avoid this comparison. Let's find our homegrown solutions. Our definition of literacy itself is embarrassing with almost no scope and hope of getting decent livelihood, why misguide the future generations into believing that Not Studying for Exam and "Failing" is OK in life. Who will feed and sustain them and their families?

Reminds me of an Interview of a young Greek Boy. He simply said that, I was all along told that' Govt will take care of us and our living expenses for life'. Suddenly, you are telling me that, I have to work and earn (time of Grexit). Neither am I prepared, nor do I have the skills to do it. My only option is to 'Play Blue Whale" unfortunately. Let's find something meaningful that will work for India and for Indian situation (Kalpen Shukla,2017).

(page purposely kept blank)

9. EDUCATION MODELS

There are various education models in the world. Every country has its own model of education that may be inspired by its own indigenous culture or motivated by cultures (behavioural pattern) of other countries. Every education model has its own legacies that has been coming out since time immemorial and even exist today in some or other form. Model may be based on primary, secondary and tertiary concept of education but common things in all such models is "teaching and learning" philosophy.

Most of the model advocates about holistic and optimistic nature of education. The following question always be at the centre of education model,

Q. How to make education simple and innovative?

Q. How to make it cost effective and within reach of people?

Q. What would be the impact of such model on societies and nature?

Q. How to make teaching and learning process simple and effective?

Q. How to provide value based education?

Q. How to produce human rather than educated man?

The objective of such models should be overall development of learner rather than cultural specific development or skill specific development. The world has been facing serious issues and challenges because of uncontrolled growth of *"obnoxious education model"* throughout the world.

The main challenge behind current model of education systems is *how to make a human being?* Most of the models of education have managed to produce machines only which is programmed for doing similar type of tasks rather than creative human full of enthusiasm and innovative ideas for delighting heart.

Old education model still have the best way to get into details of how to make the most comprehensive and competitive edge technology and ideal human being.

Whatever is happening in Finland Education System is not new, might have happened in India a long ago. But unfortunately countries like India couldn't give importance to their old glorious education system and followed the western system due to which it left behind in the race of innovative and holistic education. Still some education institutions in India and other parts of the world has been following the rich glorious system of education and able to produce holistic products. It is well said,

Creative Minds Delighted Hearts, Holistic Minds Delighted Soul.

The most important part of any model is that it must be accessible and achievable in all aspects. And every model must consist of the components of the nature education, humanities education and ethical education. All such model must aim to the goal of environmental sustainability and sustainable development of the nations and the world. It's possible that model of one country may not fit or suits to other country because of cultural backgrounds, language and geographical factors. In such cases a new model must be developed taking into account the external and internal factors which is directly or indirectly associated with teaching and learning objective. In no case models from one country need to be imposed on such countries where things are different. The new model need to be developed in consents of different stakeholders particularly representative from old age and experienced people as well as nature conservationists. It needs to be tested before implementation on ground. No model should be politically influenced and guided otherwise it will have big negative effect and impact on region or country as whole.

Reorganizing the grading system to give more weight to learning outcome of students and teachers rather than focusing on physical infrastructure of the institution. "Learning outcome remains a weak link and overall learning levels of students remain pretty disappointing. To improve the quality, physical assets need to be given just 10% weightage while 20% weightage must be given to academic assets, 30% to teacher transactions and 40% to students' learning outcome.

In order to raise the learning outcome, National Accreditation Council for Education(NACE) should conduct various assessment techniques, which include a proctored test for aspiring teachers and audio-video recording to live classroom sessions. According to the assessment, the institutes must be graded from 'A to D.' The best grade will be 'A' and the worse would be 'D'. It would be important for all the institutions to get themselves registered on the NACE website.

According to Santhosh Mathew, chairman, NCTE(National Council for Teachers Education) India, the regulations should be able control the mushrooming of poor quality institutions and bring about transparency in teachers' training. The accreditation and ranking framework of teacher education institutions should be based on physical and academic assets, teaching learning quality and learning outcome.

We find ourselves very elated at the thought no home work and no exam!

We have been adopting CBCS, CET, etc., copying a foreign model, copying only the dead skeleton and not the spirit.

Please try to understand that Philippines treat education (training of mind) as a fun: learning from within in the most natural ways, natural produce. Five senses and mind have complete autonomy to learn and enjoy the mind training. Can you think of what type of education system the country has to evolve to achieve this: natural learning like other living creatures? We need to wipe out man-made artificial education system replacing it by learning with the Nature.

If this essence or gist of education is not realized we may adopt such comfortable tools no exam but promotion to the next level, allow carry on till one touches the last pole, evaluation of students leniently, etc. Getting 100% marks or first class and above in exam as if aright will lead us to be laughable, beyond fun (P H Waghodekar'2017).

Covey defines 7 habits that lead one from dependence to independence to interdependence stage. Man is a learning animal; learning is a continuous process from birth to death, known as lifelong learning. But the life foundation is occurred mainly during the period from the childhood to adulthood; say up to the age of at the most 25 years (Brahmacharyashrama).

The learning methods and resources are obviously different from one stage to the next in fact. These stages can be classified as dependence (child depends on teacher), interdependence (adult rely on teacher and peers) and independent (self-learner adult) that in turn can be termed as pedagogy, andragogy and heutagogy respectively.

(page purposely kept blank)

Chapter 10. FRAMEWORK TO IMPLEMENT

"One nation one education is "panacea of all ills in some country: political. educational, moral, poverty, unrest/agitation, social, etc.

Abolish private sector and only keep Public sector operative or else work on PPP (Public Private Partnership).

10 years are enough to stabilize the primary public sector. If necessary, deploy all pass out graduates to this task in rural/tribal/urban areas.

Simultaneously start with overlapping planning of secondary and higher education sector with a time frame of 20 years. Do not compromise with lower target achievements, fix responsibility and teach lesson to defaulters..

Believe the cost of project can be met easily because (already State/ Central is funding to 30-40% schools in primary sector. Once the foundation is done rightly, cost of quality of education will be free because think in terms of savings in such matters as wastage reduction, unfair/corruption practices reduction, no waive of loans to farmers/business/industry/banks, etc., other social divide issues like coaching classes, private schooling, etc. would be wiped out. Varanasi social activists have recently launched a signature campaign to call for a unified primary and upper primary education in the country. The campaign has gained much momentum as of yet. One of the issues raised is to abolish the private education system. They are raising voices to have individual state boards, managed by the government, across the country under which students in the primary (1-5) and upper primary section (class five to 8) would receive common education.

They advocate that this is an essential to improve education standard at government-run-primary schools besides providing a level-playing field for students from various background.

In the state of Uttar Pradesh, there are thousands of government run schools, including primary and upper primary both. Although, when inquired about the potential plans of students once they passed class 8, the activists said the matter would be looked into once the 'one India, one education system' is implemented.

Social activist Dhananjay Tripathi said, "The national signature campaign commenced from Banaras Hindu University (BHU) gate. It is aimed at drawing the attention of government authorities towards the need for a single education system in the country."

They promote that there is an urgent need to implement 'one India, one education' system wherein it should be mandatory for all government authorities and public representatives to enroll their children in government primary schools. They also referred to the Allahabad high court order of August 2015 wherein it had instructed the chief secretary to ensure government employees, officials, people's representatives and those in judiciary send their children to government schools.

"The state government must ensure implementation of the order and come out with a plan for 'one India, one education' system," activists said.

At present there are two education systems:

    (i)   Private and
    (ii)   Public.

There is a sea of difference between the two as far as quality of education is concerned. It is an open secret that private schools are identified for imparting quality education while the quality is poor at government-run primary and upper primary schools. By implementing 'one nation, one education' system, the differences can be reduced to a great extent," Tripathi said.

The social activists took out a procession at the BHU gate, Assi ghat, Dashashwamedh ghat and other areas of the city on Friday, as part of their ongoing signature campaign. The move was to appeal people to join the signature campaign to create pressure on the government for implementation of the single education system across the country.

Including 15 BHU students, the group driving the campaign comprises 25 activists. They set their aim to cover eastern UP districts including Varanasi in the first phase of the ongoing campaign in July. Forth this, from August 1, the campaign will be launched in other parts of the state. The activists are associated with joint action committee and right to education campaign, UP (Source: The Wire).

Employees of the National Council for Teacher Education (NCTE) have recently been asked for furnish details of their income and assets, after it received several complaints of corruption against sections of staff members.

There have been complaints of corruption against employees to the council, authorised to provide recognition to B.Ed colleges and other teacher training institutes.

There have been accusations of processing recognition applications of colleges selectively.

A senior NCTE official said, "To ensure transparency and leave no scope for any act of corruption, all employees have been asked to provide details of their incomes, vehicles and properties in the past three years."

The details, as per officials, were sought from the employees in the past too. Now, although, it has been made mandatory commission's website will soon put up the details.

Back in 2015, the Lok Sabha had been informed by the then HRD Minister Smriti Irani, of the establishment of a vigilance wing designed to look into complaints of corruption against NCTE officials (Source: PTI).

As per Terence Mauri, author of "The Leader's Mindset: How to Win in the Age of Disruption", future-proofing companies will require significant mindset shifts from:

- profit to purpose,
- hierarchies to networks,
- controlling to collaborating,
- planning to experimentation and
- privacy to transparency

His advice includes:

- Incentivise risk and experimentation.
- Fail wisely and avoid the status quo.

The world is becoming an increasingly difficult entity to predict. Business, economy, politics and society are part of the same ecosystem, certainly, but the rules of engagement have changed and what held well once upon a time is no longer good enough. The future of the VUCA (volatile, uncertain, complex and ambiguous) world is completely different and its challenges, unprecedented. Disruptive technologies and the internet are driving these changes and it takes not only a well-informed manager to understand the implications, but a smart one to be able to realise the potential of such disruptions.

Educators therefore, have a duty to offer knowledge not only for the basic understanding and appreciation of the discipline but also for enhancing skillsets and expertise that will help the students face up to the challenges of the coming years. In this context, the higher education segment has a crucial role to play.

Here is a summary of some of the things that are wrong with management education in India and some suggested remedies (Prof. Balachandran Bala V.):

Lack of qualified faculty: While the regulatory authorities impose specific mandatory requirements for appointing qualified faculty members and principals, the word 'quality' is a tricky one. There is a huge variance in the quality of the qualifications that a person in the world can acquire. You cannot equate a good Ph.D. obtained through rigorous research work from accredited university with the one obtained from a fly-by-night school/institute/university or some private educational institute/ university which focuses merely on *earning* than learning. However, both candidates can certainly be appointed professors since they do have the requisite Ph.D. qualification. One way to handle is to use the philosophy of "publish or perish" which will ensure that there is an emphasis on research output even after the Ph.D. has been obtained. One might argue that there are unverified and dubious "online" journals in which one could publish and once again quality will be suspect. Institutes need to insist on research and paper publications only in rated and peer reviewed journals. This will ensure quality and therefore equality in the overall standards of qualification.

The low financial packages in the education sector vis-à-vis the Industry: The pay and perks that many faculties get in India are not commensurate with rest of the world or even the rest of Asia. Faculty members have to become a "teaching machine" or take on "forced consulting" to generate the income needed to sustain a comfortable lifestyle and send their children to good schools. Thus, the effectiveness of their overall academic performance suffers. The package should be on par with the opportunity cost of having worked in the corporate domain. Ensuring decent package and providing incentives for scholarly work and effective performance are essential.

NO discipline: The unfortunate reality that is being seen in today's society is the general disregard for discipline and ethical values. Let's be clear that without either, there is no success or achievement whether personal or professional. Teachers and parents especially in the 'K to 12' age group have to do their bit in moulding the youth with these fundamental strengths. Collegiate and higher education should certainly reinforce these qualities and this is the only way to create super-performers who are also responsible corporate citizens.

Merit should prevail: Reservation should not take precedence over merit. If the government ensures access to basic, good and free education to all right from kindergarten the quota systems won't be necessary in higher education. The merit system has to supersede and include standardised tests as well as an overall assessment of the achievements, quality and potential of the student leaving no room for subjective interpretation. No student is 'unfit' but there may be 'misfits'. Everyone need not be a "book smart" person but can be "streetsmart".

Experiential learning: We need to focus on experiential learning besides class room teaching. Integrated and energised teaching should be encouraged. Also a questioning attitude among students must be encouraged and exams need to test that. The evaluation system currently encourages the students to master the 'art of cheating' as opposed to the 'science of teaching'.

Faculty members: Every class should have two faculty — one from industry stressing the business relevance and an academic who can bring "academic elegance" — the fundamental concepts and discipline of the subject. This way the shortage of academics can be filled to an extent with industry experts in an environment where the art of Leadership blends with the science of management. This is another way to ensure that the teachers are brought up to speed and they continue to learn.

In sum, several mandatory changes are required in the way that management education is delivered in India. More so since the avenues for gaining said knowledge are going to multiply in the coming years. The faculty members are neither challenged intellectually nor are they financially motivated to engage in research. Evaluation methods are compromised and experiential learning is close to zero. If this continues, there will be a large number of textbook managers who won't have the resourcefulness to excel in business and society. It is time to embrace the change.

Digital India looks forward to this great initiative indeed to pave the way for inclusive education for a vast country like ours with diverse training needs of huge number of cohorts and regional clusters of 15 to 35 age group groping for skill-enhancement for their livelihood.

Every Higher-Education institute needs to have its In-house-Mobile-Swayam-Platform using Distributed Ledger Technology DLT (block chain) for executing Teaching-Learning-Contract with the students registered with them.

Rapid and innovative content-development (over and above the Free Sessions) and its content-ownership issues will be monitored and addressed with time-stamped academic administration through DLT.

Personalized systems of instructions need to be developed in education.

The education of every student must be individualized to help all students achieve success and realize their highest potential.

The learning environment indeed needs to be centered on student needs and academic preparation, all pointing toward the goal of acquiring workplace values, developing life skills, and realizing professional aspirations.

The intentional focus on career preparation motivates students to create professional growth plans and monitor their progress as they build positive self-images.

The instructors may have to be proactive in the engagement and advancement of all students, providing them with extra time and assistance as needed, designing multiple opportunities for students to demonstrate their knowledge, and offering advanced students chances to explore course content in greater depth.

SUGGESTIVE FRAMEWORK

Significant policy initiatives, such as welcoming of private education sectors in the country, foreign and Diasporas investments must be looked upon. Educationist must be given opportunity and assistance to run education programmes without imposing burdens of unnecessary rules regulations and related expenses. Following steps would be of great help;

- Setting up of the World Education Monetary Foundation

(WEMF for rendering financial assistance & launching new projects, monitoring the programmes and catering to other needs of Asian-Pacific. WEMF would be of great help in this direction.

- Government and non-government education agencies should wake up to the need to work closely in partnership on the issue of conservation of environment , forests, coastal areas, tribal belts, hills as well as other flora and fauna. And for this they must prepare a common curriculum.

- Guidelines should be framed under which all education projects have to get all types of clearance certificate whatsoever reason may be without any delay and hindrances. Today conservationists, economists and tourists alike have awakened to the realization that you can't save nature and monuments at the expense of local people. They are the traditional and time honored custodians of the land and are most likely to lose from conservation and should be convinced that they are the beneficiaries and partners in conservation rather than enemies of it. Therefore Government of these countries should empower the local people through education and necessary assistance should be provided in terms of money, materials, methods, technology, training & development as well as employment. International policies and guidelines are required for easy formalities and jointly sharing the whole education system for getting more benefits out of it.

- Convenient accessibility for the education purposes to be made available for education seekers, no matter he/she belongs to which class, religion, castes, tribes, zone and income group. Procedure should be fair enough in all the zones and it should not be a bad dream for any one.

- Unnecessary rules and regulations should be abolished and some common education policies need to be laid down on the basis of common consensus by organizing meeting and conference.

- For boosting the education system rationalization of open learning is required, rules and regulations must be framed in framed for the benefits of all that is from grass root level to top.

- Establishment of holistic (emphasized conservation of nature, environment and humanity, culture, wildlife, and other scarce resources) based educational institution, training centres and a Regulatory body to control and monitor the condition of workers, professionals and independent entrepreneurs is required on urgent basis to solve the problems of exploitation and survival.

- Political realignment in the South Asian Country particularly for neighboring country of India as free education zone will encourage travel within each region.

(page purposely kept blank)

Chapter 11. HI-TECH EDUCATION AND SMART EDUCATION

Modern technology has brought phenomenal changes in the delivery mechanism of teaching and learning system. Latest computerized technologies have given new dimensions to the classrooms. And classrooms have become more versatile and interactive due to scope of exploring the things in more practical way by introducing the live examples from real life situations and business environment. Visualization of things has been increased from merely to listening. And now complicated calculations can be done within fraction of seconds.

Different types of software are being used for data analysis and interpretation and preparing various types of need based reports. Parents could see the performance of their wards by sitting far from the place of residence and can give feedback online. Internet has provided flexibility to both teachers and students in day to day communication to resolve the issues and clear the doubts. School, colleges and universities have been working more efficiently in terms of managing administrative works and coordination for exchanging various crucial information. Now conducting examinations and publishing results on time hasn't been any more than just a matter of click on mouse button.

Technology has paved the way of doing the job easily just because it is convenient and resourceful.

11.1. Applications of Technology in Education

(I) Teaching and Learning

(II) Module Preparation

(III) Lecture Presentation

(IV) Seminars Conferences and Meeting

(V) Research and Development

(VI) Training and Placement

(VII) Career Counselling

(VIII) Communication

(IX) Students Profile Management and Counselling

(X) Grade Card and Report Generation

(XI) Feedback Analysis

(XII) Accreditation and Affiliation

(XIII) Library Management

(XIV) Cultural Programs and Youth Festivals

(XV) Teleconference and Webinars

(XVI) Language Translation

The above mentioned are some of the most important applications of technology but not limited to this. Modern technology has speedup the growth of education and been contributing tremendous in distance and online digital education. Multimedia has provided a broader scope to open education system through interactive teleconference. The cost of education will be low through online universities. Besides, the quality will be at par with physical ones. Moreover, with this initiative, we can compel students, who leave studies after school, to study further. One can even work while studying with such universities.

Also, this will be beneficial in places where basic high-level education infrastructure is not up to the mark.

New technology of 2100 AD functioning through chips/ buttons of human body.

11.2. Technology Disadvantages

Modern technology has many disadvantages as it doesn't allow students and teachers to explore their creativity and innovativeness because of comfort zones. It restricts the complete utilization of human brain and breeds the attitude of short cuts theory in life. It has killed the conceptualizing ability of most of the human beings due to availability of data at one click options. Global warming, climate change, terror attacks in schools and colleges, econometrics of bomb-war and other social and environmental degradation have been happening because of the misuse of technology.

ILLUSTRATION- I

EDUTECH: The Future of India Education

(Source: Venguswamy Ramaswamy, Global Head of TCS, a Tata Consultancy Services unit focused on Education, Assessment Boards and SMBs)

The Indian education sector is witnessing a continuous transformation brought about by technology and these variations are influencing its key stakeholders in multifarious ways. From helping students to learn more and better anytime anywhere, empowering teachers to develop innovative instructional aids and methods, to driving educational institutes to cross the digital divide – technology is underpinning the Edutech revolution in India.

Let us see how this transformation is affecting key communities:

1. For students: A new world of learning

Web-based content consumption to get a boost: Laptop-based or mobile-based models will be the preferred gadget solutions for leveraging content even as the number of students using tablets will witness a downturn. Mobile, with the multiple advantages it offers, and desktops/laptops, with the ease of consumption it guarantees, will continue to rule the roost. The trend will gain further momentum in 2018.

Engaging content: With the change in content itself, India is set to see a trend of a mobile-ready, gamified, interactive and engaged content. This kind of content consumption will change the way students learn. Adaptive learning will gain traction as it will personalize learning material based on their learning speed, interest and problem areas.

English content still ruling the industry: English will not only be the preferred medium of coaching but we will also witness an upswing in the quantum and quality of content being offered in English. While the demand for content in vernacular languages will register an upswing, the offerings will remain negligible compared to English. To bridge the demand-availability gap, trainers / teachers will be forced to use English content but instruct in local languages.

Social learning: Learning with and from others either online or offline – will become a dominant trend in the coming years. 24×7 learning resources which go beyond classroom environment and enable students to learn anywhere, anytime will be mainstream.

User validated content to become mainstream: With content options set to increase exponentially, students and other users are likely to begin relying on user-validated content to find correct and meaningful information. Higher the validation, proportionate will be the relevance and accuracy of content for users searching for it. This year will also witness more R&D on applications that help users to navigate through the data overload; however, the trend will take another 3-4 years to become mainstream.

Impressive resumes: India is all set to become the world's youngest country by 2020 with 64 per cent of its population in the working age group. With an increasing number of graduates entering the market every day and limited job opportunities, only those with value-added resumes will pass muster with businesses and employers. Resumes that boast of additional certifications, proficiency in international languages and other allied qualifications will have an edge over plain-vanilla ones.

> 2. *For teachers: Digital natives to lead*

Technology the need of the hour: Digital native teachers proficient with digital technologies and systems will be the mascots for the new-age teacher-facilitator. Digital immigrants will be forced to change and embrace technology to remain relevant.

Teachers to become facilitators: From teacher as the 'sage on the stage', their role will evolve into that of a 'guide on the side'. Teachers will increasingly become facilitators who will help students to learn rather than tutor them as is the norm currently. While the trend is picking up, it will take some time to become ubiquitous.

Improving and developing curriculum with the use of technology: The teacher as an educational visionary will embrace technology to research and create lessons that complement / supplement the curriculum. However, this trend will take time to become mainstream phenomenon.

> 3. *For administrators: Embracing a new digital era*

Existing content to be digitized: Indian universities will step-up digitization efforts in 2018. In the near term, institutions will focus more on digitizing existing content to make it available to attract a wider reach of students in a cost-effective manner.

Different approach to way of learning & assessments: Flipped classrooms, combining online and offline modes of learning will increasingly become the norm. Concurrently, institutions will also step up efforts to move from paper-pencil based assessments to digital assessments. The increasing thrust on digitization will also compel coaching institutes, which train students for competitive exams, to follow suit.

Digital campuses to gain ground: The 'go digital' campaign will spur educational institutions to digitally revamp existing business processes such as admission procedures, grading, library, accounts, etc. With most institutes of higher education having failed to meet the objectives of the Action Plan 17-by-17 for Digital Campuses enumerated by the Government of India, efforts to jumpstart the process will gain ground in 2018.

VR, AR and augmented reality set to get more potent: Virtual reality, augmented reality and artificial intelligence-based platforms are still 2-3 years away from becoming ubiquitous in learning. However, the trend will get more potent in 2018 as customers and companies will continue to invest in capabilities and systems which will in the future disrupt traditional methods and pedagogies.

With students, educators and administrators embracing the digital revolution, classrooms and learning are set to change for good.

11.4. Conclusion

Hi-Tech and smart education has become an integral part of modern education system. These hi-tech classrooms provides tremendous and diversified opportunities to explore the things in simple and detailed ways without losing the seconds. But at the same time supressed the growth of brain and its conceptualizing ability. Students becomes addicted to easy to go platform and doesn't utilise the full capacity of brain due to which innovations becomes challenge.

Smart classrooms and hi-tech education must be used to brain storming rather than brain washing. Teacher must be trained psychologically to understand the needs and judge through the behaviour of students in such classrooms. Parents must take responsibility to keep eye on the activities and usage of smartphones or hi-tech gadgets by their wards. Positive and negative effect must be analysed to come out on any conclusion and then remedial measures must be taken to compensate the loss or damage to brain (innovation).

Educational institutions must be interfaced with parents to practice the best smart classrooms technology. Regular counselling and demonstrations need to be done on the application, advantage and disadvantages of hi-tech gadgets for students, parents and teachers.

Technology is important as it is outcome of human brain only but it should not be the reason of draining hundreds of brain rather than sharpening the brain. The best way to adopt the adaptive management in classrooms to improve the things through the outcomes of classroom management.

(page purposely kept blank)

Chapter

12. EDUCATION TOURISM

Tourism is interlinked with education as tourists travel to learn and gain experience from host communities and tourism destinations. These learning experiences are mostly intangible, perishable and heterogeneous in nature that needs to be satisfactory. The main motive behind tourism is to observe and learn the cultural attributes of host communities and natural settings. The quest of finding new things, new knowledge and peaceful happiness motivates people to take tourism trip.

Tourism is a process of experiencing change through journey from place of origin to destination leading to peaceful happiness and eternal satisfaction of travellers / visitors and other forms of tourists. Natural and cultural diversity are the prime factors that are associated with the phenomenon of tourism. However factors like spiritual odyssey, metaphysical and other scientific aspects leading to research and self-recognition can't be ignored.

Education on other hand is process of learning from environment and communities to satisfy the quest and develop ability to differentiate between good and evil. Education is the tool through which an animal can be trained to become social animal and inhuman could become human.

More you travel, more you learn, more you become educated, and more you contribute in transformation of yourself and others in line with environment. The real essence of education is sustainable development with peace and harmony. Travelling is directly linked with tourism and education as well. Tourism has various forms and each form has educational component based on real time environment and situations. These components are dynamic and versatile like education which makes it interlinked and intertwined.

Tourism has socio-economic and socio-cultural impacts which further integrate with nation building activities.

(page purposely kept blank)

Chapter

13. CONCLUSION AND ROAD MAP

There is an urgent need to develop a new learning curriculum and technology to cover the entire educational spectrum of the country to meet with world spectrum. The continuous research work will find the ways of expanding the education network at regional and central level.

Open and distance learning is by far the most effective method to reach a maximum numbers of people and deliver a top-quality job oriented courses and training programme at an affordable cost. This is the only way by which we can reach five times as many people through self-study distance learning as through traditional classroom courses and in any other training programme.

We will have to make sure that the growth in this field will be remained continue till the target of 100% literacy and employment for everyone is achieved. The latest teaching trends and technology by which we can reach to the ultimate target segment must be adopted to reach out the maximum. In present scenario of technology we should go for the use of e-learning as a tool for effective learning and training. The government has to show the way to expand and build networks of partners with new organization such as NGO's and other Governmental Organizations.

The promotion of education is deeply affected by the social, technological, and economic factors. Therefore all these factors should be given due credit in the research. Government Policies provides a basis framework which minds and controls every aspects of Education. Therefore, it has to be studied regularly so that not a single factor remains untouched. For the development and promotion of any aspect of education the basic infrastructural facilities are very important. Therefore it has to be taken into consideration while planning the aspect.

Strength and weakness need to be identified and must be given due consideration to improve the system. The main objective must lies on democratizing education by taking it to the doorsteps of the learners. Providing high quality education to all those who seek it irrespective of age, sex, region, class, caste or religion and formal qualification. The Government and controlling authorities should take necessary initiatives and actions to improve the qualities and modes of open and distance learning systems to speed up the process of transformations of conventional system into open and distance mode on a large scale.

Open education and distance learning is a boon for backward class people of India for whom education is a dream. No doubt in this that open learning and distance mode of education has power to reach at the maximum people in minimum time and less cost but establishing study centres across the nation particularly in remotest areas is a big responsibility on the shoulder of educationist and reformist. The open system of education allows people of different ages, sex and religion to come on common platform to gain and share the knowledge and skills without any hesitation and shy.

A time will come when the dream of 100% literacy would become true due to open and distance system of learning but for that we must keep on putting our right efforts rigorously and regularly. Education has tremendous power to show, only when it is explored and exhibited.

Open learning has tremendous power to generate awareness among local communities whereas distance education mode has capacity to facilitate various programmes directly to the learner at their own place or very near to place of resident hence, it provides opportunity to implement the learning outcomes on ground reality which may become effective in true sense as learner is very much known to the local communities and also he/she has high level of understanding regarding his/her place and community.

FRAMEWORK - 1

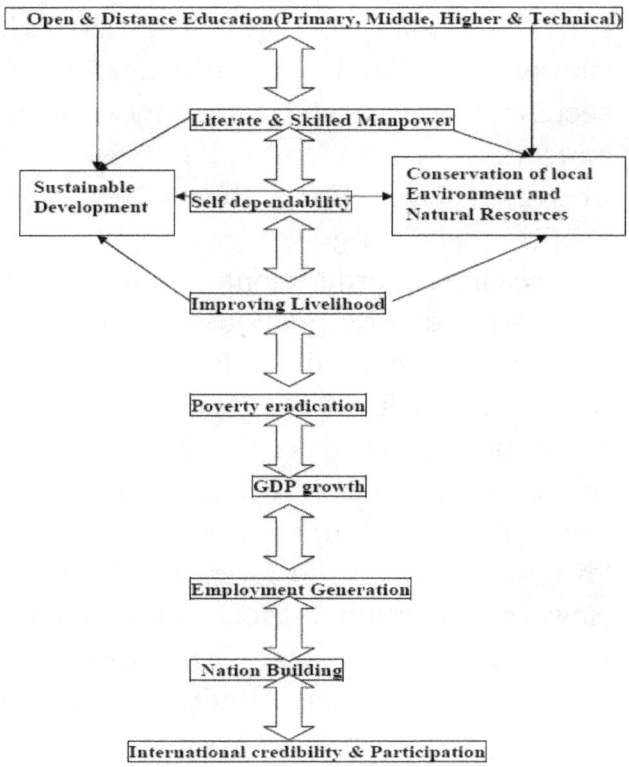

Moral Education and Secular Ethics Development through Open Education System:

Education for sustainable development is very serious matter not only for developing professionalism but also for other ideal citizen. It should follow a proper secular ethics and moral values. According to spiritual leader and Nobel peace prize winner, Dalai Lama, moral education and secular ethics must be introduced in the education system from kindergarten to university level. Then there's real hope. People becoming judges, politicians, businessmen, professionals, and leaders will have a different way of thinking. Then society will be totally different(Times of India dt.3rd Feb.'2012). According to him some people feel moral ethics must be based on religious principles. All religious traditions carry moral principles based on love, compassion, forgiveness, tolerance. However, in reality, the number of non-believers is quite big. Even those who claim to be Buddhist, Hindu, Christian or other religions may not be very serious about these teachings in their daily lives. We need to promote moral ethics, but for your own interest, your family's interest and for the sake of the community, we need secular ethics.

People must be taught about inner potential- real source of inner peace, self-confidence and inner strength. And in this direction Open learning and distance mode of education may become important method to reach out to maximum number of people with an effective curriculum. And it will help Asia-Pacific countries to come more closure.

(Page purposely kept blank)

ANNEXURE- I

Cell Phone Etiquette

More cell phone etiquette is needed than for **any other** type of communication device.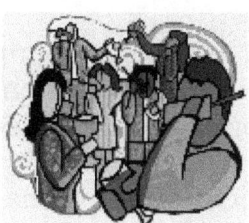

Cell phones, being mobile, are often used in situations where the **phone user** and the conversation are **not welcome.**

Their use in some venues may be considered rude and even downright **offensive.**

Almost all the tips on telephone etiquette apply to cell phones with the addition of one very important one – don't contribute to **noise pollution.**

There is no doubt that cell phones have a permanent and **essential** role in modern society.

But when cell phones interrupt important proceedings and are used in the **wrong place** at the **wrong time,** it is unacceptable and makes us grind our teeth in despair at the users' rudeness and blatant lack of care **and** consideration for the people around them.

The following are some of the places and events where cell phones should be **switched off** or the ring tone muted.

If it is vitally important to be reached in such places then the call should be kept brief **and** the voice low:

- On public transport in proximity to other commuters

- In hospitals, restaurants and shopping centres

- At checkouts, cinemas and theatres

- Train stations, bus stops and air ports

- Doctors' surgeries, churches and conventions

- Waiting rooms, libraries and lecture rooms

- At christenings, weddings and funerals

- And at a dozen other places that you can think of without my help

It's **not the use** of cell phones that is the problem; it's the loud and annoying ring tone.

It's the **shouting** into the cell phone; it's the airing of one's **private life** on the cell phone in the presence of strangers.

It's the endless **verbal diarrhoea** and ear bashing that one and all are subjected to without fear or favour that is the problem.

Driving **or** walking on the street while talking on the mobile phone delays the reflexes and can shorten someone's life.

That life could be yours. So **be safe** or be sorry.

It is bad cell phone etiquette to make a call whilst **in the company** of another person.

In fact, it is downright **rude.**

If you absolutely must make that call, **apologise** first, and then make the call.

Keep it very **brief.**

Sending **text messages** in company is even worse.

Once again, if you must, **excuse** yourself first and then be very brief.

Share the message with those present as a courtesy to let them know that they are not the subject of the message.

It is **unforgiveable** to talk on a mobile phone while 'dealing' with another person such as a checkout in a shop or bank-teller or greeting or farewelling someone.

Lastly, **camera** cell phones. These are so useful and handy.

Be aware of privacy laws, the **rights** of others and charges of voyeurism if used inappropriately in the wrong places.

Practicing good cell phone etiquette will **not** improve your popularity but it will certainly not make you **unpopular.**

Importantly, you will not be contributing to **cell phone rage.**

****

REFERENCES

- http://accomplishedteacher.org/wp-content/uploads/2017/02/EAYA-CTE.pdf
- http://www.3boxsolution.com/author/ Focus on "three-box" leadership proposed by Vijay Govindarajan,
- http://www.a-to-z-of-manners-and-etiquette.com/cell-phone-etiquette.html /21/10/2015 PHW
- http://www.indianex press.com/news/the- higher-education -myth/931269/ 06/04/2012
- http://www.news-gazette.com/news/local/2017-10-29/cellphones-get-ringing-endorsement-classrooms.html/31/10/2017 PHW
- http://www.teachthought.com/pedagogy/a-primer-in-heutagogy-and-self-directed-learning/
- https://www.teachthought.com/category/learning-models/
- ISRO chairman G Madhavan Nair ,July' 2017,Education has become a commercial commodity, An Interview on NDTV, India

- Kumar C., 2016, A Conman in Solitary Confinement, Vol-I, CreateSpace, amazon.com, USA
- Kumar C., 2016, Pandava of Modern Times on Intellectual Lines, (A conman in Solitary Confinement , Vol-II), CreateSpace, amazon.com, USA
- Kumar C., Aditi C., Kulshrestha S., (2013) Open Learning System and Distance Education mode for Sustainable Development of Tourism to Transform India in Book title Tourism Education and Future Initiative, Jnanada Prakashan, New Delhi, India,Chapter-4, Pg.-71-89.
- MTC Global, Googlegroups.

******

www.ingramcontent.com/pod-product-compliance
Lightning Source LLC
Chambersburg PA
CBHW031442040426
42444CB00007B/935